BOOK OF SUCCESSFUL PAINTING

BOOK OF SUCCESSFUL PAINTING

by Abel Banov with Marie-Jeanne Lytle

Structures Publishing Company
Farmington, Michigan 1975

Manufactured in the United States of America

Book designed by Richard Kinney

Current Printing (last digit)
10 9 8 7 6 5 4 3 2

International Standard Book Number: 0-912336-36-6 (hardcover)

Library of Congress Catalog Card Number: 74–21836

Structures Publishing Co.
Box 423, Farmington, Mich. 48024

COVER PHOTO BY HEDRICH-BLESSING, CHICAGO

Photos attributed to Carpet and Rug Institute
from Carpet and Rug Institute, Dalton, Ga. 30720

CONTENTS

INTRODUCTION

Now that real estate values have climbed beyond most people's dreams, interest has naturally heightened among responsible owners in maintaining the value of their property by proper care.

Few details of maintenance rank with painting both as to cost and importance. When paint deteriorates, the house looks terrible. If enough houses in a neighborhood are unsightly, pride evaporates and those desirable neighbors with well-kept houses soon leave. So the cost and bother of keeping a house well-painted has dividends for the owner that are both visible and invisible.

Keeping the cost of painting—and the bother—to reasonable levels is the purpose of this book. Far too many people fail to understand that painting a house properly is no more troublesome than doing it in a clownish fashion. Regarding a paint job as something you do with brawn and no brains is likely to result in the use of far more brawn more frequently and in the more frequent outlay of money for material and labor, either the kind you hire or your own.

Therefore, it pays to do it right. This usually results in doing it less often; and no one objects to that.

The plan of ''The Book of Successful Painting'' is to start off with color schemes and their selection, then go on to an analysis of the causes of failure in painting, and then proceed to study how to prepare surfaces for painting as the professional painters do. With the most important aspects—recognizing the causes of trouble and how to overcome them—out of the way, the fourth chapter reviews how to set up for painting, followed by a chapter on the methods of actual application.

In the sequence of steps in a painting operation, we put the first

thing last, *selecting the right coating*. We do this because we want to discourage the notion that paint is the most important factor in painting. It is merely important. Surface preparation and understanding the cause of failure are equally important; but since this is not generally understood, they have received greater emphasis here.

The final chapter is devoted to refinishing objects around the house.

Professional methods, in all instances, are put forward here. Most of the material comes from "Paints and Coatings Handbook," written for architects, engineers and contractors, by one of the authors. The big difference between the two books is that the original includes instructions for coating numerous surfaces requiring materials and methods of little interest to the general consumer. Those portions of value to the homeowner have been included in full detail.

To use this book efficiently, refer to the Table of Contents to learn the whereabouts of general subjects. For specific problems or for information about coating specific surfaces under certain circumstances, consult the Subject Index in the back of the book.

1

How to Select the Color

by Marie-Jeanne Lytle*

So you are going to paint! You won't simply run down to the paint store and buy some paint. Later chapters will discuss what *kind* of paint to buy; how to *prepare the surface;* and how to apply it. But before you do all that, you must consider what you want the colors to do; the emotions and symbolism you want to evoke; the illusions you hope to create; the color scheme; and finally the color, but along with color you need to decide the *hue, value* and *intensity.* This chapter, then, is your first step.

Color is a whole new world today. New paints, plastics, synthetics and fibers have expanded the range of colors enormously and new ones are coming every day. There are no restrictions—only your own preferences and choices.

There is no longer any reason to retreat to a safe color scheme following the old rigid rules of color combinations and color matching. You can experiment—the expense of redecorating and the amount of time required for a new coat of paint is minimal compared to the fixed and expensive decorating of the past.

Tired of a color scheme in a room? Change it! Color is now employed to a much greater degree for quick, short-term effects.

At the same time, color is more important than ever before. In our modern, look-alike, space-starved apartments and houses, decoration is left almost entirely to color. We rarely have the architectural features of the rooms of the past (the bay windows, the nooks and crannies,

*Marie-Jeanne Lytle studied art at the University of Chicago. After being a decorator for Marshall Field & Co., she was Midwest Decorating Editor for "Living for Young Homemakers" magazine. Since becoming a fulltime housewife, she has maintained her interest in decorating and art. Marie-Jeanne is the co-author of "Book of Successful Fireplaces."

8

One whole wall is painted gold, while the others are white . . . and the effect is added width to a narrow room . . . also a feeling of limitless space in the white areas. An extremely good example of the effective use of color. (Photographed at Sea Colony Development, Bethany Beach, Del.; Hedrich-Blessing Photo) the wainscoting, the chair rails). We need color badly to add interest and change the shape of box-like rooms.

We can even perform color sleight-of-hand to make something out of the "blah" nothing room or the badly-designed space. The "trompe l'oeil" (fool the eye) technique of painting can be used in room decoration to produce whatever illusion is needed.

So we have space to decorate—with color and illusions to create with paint. Where do we begin?

First, look at the problem and analyze it. What is the space to be used for—bedroom, family room, office? What are its characteristics—is it too small, too large, too narrow, too dull? Where is it located—on the north or south side of the building? All of these factors will have an effect upon your choice of color.

There are some rough guidelines. Bedrooms can represent personal color preference, but in the family room, the colors must be acceptable to all the family. An entrance hall can be exciting and startling in color, because it is a small space and the amount of time spent in it short.

An office or a waiting room, on the other hand, should be calm and undistracting. An executive's private office can reflect that particular individual's taste, but a large office requires a more universally appealing color scheme—one that will be soothing to the eyes and conducive to cheerful efficiency. An important factor here is to check out the colors with the existing lighting, under regular office conditions of artificial (and natural, if any) light.

People differ in their color likes and dislikes and the people using your space must be taken into account. Children, as infants, see only bright colors first and through their early years prefer light, bright, warm colors. Adults become more subtle in their preferences.

And, last but not least, there must be some thought for the existing colors surrounding the space—some sort of general overall color plan into which the particular room you are decorating fits.

Now that you have focused on the problem, there are tools to help you. One of these tools is the psychology of color. Color evokes emotion and certain colors have definite appeal to certain personalities:

		Have these qualities:	Are preferred by people who are:
Warm colors	Red Orange Yellow	Busy Happy Bright Stimulating Cheerful	Emotional Vigorous Extroverted More Social Active
Cool Colors	Green Blue Violet	Relaxing Soft Depressing Sad Quiet	Introverted More interested in self than the world Passive Solemn

9

And then there is the symbolism of color—certain colors bring to mind certain things. Here are some examples of color symbolism:

White.   Innocence, joy, purity, glory

Red.   Fire, blood, passion, danger, Christmas, Valentine's Day

Yellow.   Alertness, intellectual, joyous, cowardice.

Blue.   Sedation, conservative, calm, cold, remote, pure

Green.   Nature, cool, fresh, St. Patrick's Day, tranquillity

Purple.   Royalty, melancholy, sophistication, Easter

Orange.   Friendly, Thanksgiving and Halloween.

Color can create optical illusions. Warm colors (Red, Orange and Yellow) appear to *advance* and cool colors (Blue, Green and Violet) appear to *recede.* If you have a long, narrow room, the use of bright warm colors on the end walls and white on the long side walls will tend to equalize things. If you have a room that is large and barn-like, then the walls in a darker tone of a warm color will make it seem smaller and more friendly.

A long corridor can be shortened visually by painting the end walls a bright, warm color. Interest can be gained by painting the doors in the corridor different bright colors.

Light colors appear lighter in weight than dark colors. This applies particularly in the selection of ceiling and floor colors. The use of a black ceiling in a room with white walls and white carpeting is certainly going to appear top-heavy! On the other hand, if you have a very high ceiling, the use of a darker shade of the wall color, for instance, will make it seem lower and cozier in feeling.

The old rigid rules of color combinations and color matching are now disregarded, but the *Color Wheel* (Page 18), based on the order in which colors appear when light is refracted through a prism, is still a valuable tool in visualizing color relationships.

The words employed by professionals to express the mystique and workings of a color often sound more complicated than they are. Here are some useful definitions of the properties of color:

Hue.   The name of the color

Value.   A measure of whether a color is light or dark.

Intensity.   A measure of the brightness or dullness of a color.

Monochromatic, analogous, complementary, split-complementary, analogous-complementary, and triadic are technical terms that describe combinations taken from the Color Wheel.

Color schemes are merely guideposts. After you have learned the rules, you can stretch and break them.

Here are the major color schemes:

10   1. *The Neutrals*—one or two colors with black, white, beige, or gray,

or any of the metallics (silver, gold, copper, etc.) . . . the simplest of all. Walls might be white, sofa a medium blue, white and olive green print, chairs in the green, and the carpet a white shag with flecks of green. Another combination could be white walls with a black and white squared tiled floor. Add a bright yellow sofa and chairs and you have a striking porch or Florida room.

Major schemes for color are illustrated on the color wheel drawings below. These are merely guideposts which you can adapt after you have learned the rules.

2. *The Monochromatic Scheme*—one in which many shades of a single color are used, simple and attractive. Walls might be pale, pale pink, woodwork and carpeting a medium shade of pink, and the bedspread and chairs in hot pink. In order to relieve possible monotony, the use of black and white accents and a variation of textures are helpful here.

3. *The Analogous Scheme*—uses colors which adjoin each other on the color wheel, such as yellow, yellow-green and green, or red, red-orange, and orange. These colors usually are not in their pure form, rather in varying values and intensities, but usually one of the colors predominates.

3.

4. *Analogous Scheme with Complementary Accent*—an analogous scheme accented by a color that is opposite on the color wheel. For example, a yellow-green, green and blue-green color scheme with accents of red.

4.

5. *Complementary Scheme*—in its basic form, two colors opposite each other on the color wheel, such as blue-green and red-orange. Each color makes the other look more attractive and mixed together they give a neutral gray, which indicates a perfect balance. (In vision, green is the after-image of red . . . operating rooms and the robes of the doctors and nurses are green in order to minimize eye fatigue.)

5.

6. *Near, or Split Complements*—a split complement takes the form of a Y on the color wheel, the one arm of the Y pointing, for instance, to yellow-orange, the other to red-orange and the stem to blue.

6.

7. *Double-Split Complement*—takes the form of an X on the color wheel. For example, the top legs point to yellow-orange and red-orange and the bottom legs to blue-green and blue-violet.

7.

8. *Triad*—an excellent color scheme which mixes the three colors located at the third points of the wheel, such as red, blue and yellow. It offers a wide range of hues, values and intensities, such as muted tones for the traditional look and vibrant colors for the modern look.

11

8.

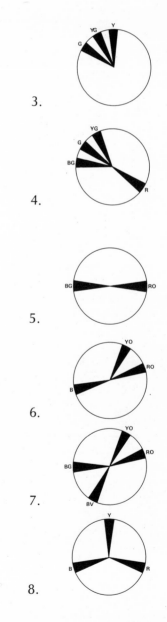

White, of course, is the lightest of the neutrals and the color most universally relied upon to accent, punctuate or relieve a color scheme. Next to white and the neutrals, the simplest color scheme to handle is monochromatic, darkened by black or dark neutrals, lightened by white or pale neutrals.

One of the most recent developments in color popularity has been the OP colors. OP colors are used to create optical illusions or effects, causing movements of the eye. For slow movements, use complementary colors. For fast movements, dissonant colors are used.

OP colors are strong primary and secondary colors of the spectrum, such as red, blue, orange, and purple juxtaposed in clashing combinations that have a visual effect of seeming to move. Along with the OP colors come free designs that move from wall to wall and from floor to ceiling. It is the old trompe l'oeil all over again. It directs the eye around the room, hides architectural deformities from view, creates headboards or other interest where there was none before and is a fascinating new method of creating an individual living space out of modern cubicles.

We cannot ignore those among us who wish to reconstruct exactly the period of history in which they would prefer to live. Period color lines are created by paint companies for both interior and exterior, and they are well researched and presented. Williamsburg Green and Sutton's Gold, Early American Turkey Red, Pompeian Red, French Blue and so on are classic colors that have stood the test of time and are always pleasing.

If you have a beautiful collection of blue and white Chinese porcelains, brown and white Benningtonware, a favorite painting or print, a great colorful fabric . . . all of these can help you create a striking individual personal color scheme for your room. Follow the guidelines and you are all set.

Color schemes for the home should be easy on the eyes. Determine the color that will be used in each part of the room and decide on their intensities. Color balance must be achieved by carefully selecting areas and volumes that are to be light, dark, pale, or intense in color.

Colors should never be strewn around wholesale—they cancel each other out. A needless contrast, such as black ceiling and walls with a white carpet on the floor, is unnatural and annoying to the eye. Always consider where you want attention to be focussed—on a seating area, a particular painting or piece of furniture, or a fireplace—and then call on color to pull it off.

Half of the success of decorating with color is seeing the elements and areas of a room from a different and more precise vantage point. To size them up, pretend you are a camera. Focus on one wall, object, or corner. Visualize how it would look in a bright new guise. This is the reason for the painted accent piece or wall. By directing the eye toward a specific thing, you can distract it from any architectural mistake better ignored.

By adding a new visual dimension, color can overcome such architectural liabilities as the "problem" door, beam, or window, even exposed piping. The trend now is to accept, even to glorify them with color.

Exteriors

This discussion would seem to deal only with interior room decoration. However—all of the color principles apply with equal force to exterior paint decisions.

In planning a color scheme for the exterior of the home, you must have a starting point. This logically could be the roof, since its material usually cannot be painted and the color remains unchanged. A near-white roof will reflect the heat of the sun in the summer—an important factor to consider.

Another "unchangeable" factor which affects your color decision are the houses on either side, if they are close. You may wish to be adventurous, but the result is not likely to be happy if your choice "fights" with your neighbors' homes.

Well-designed doorways, window boxes, and shutters are areas where you can have interesting color accents. These are especially important in areas where all the homes are of similar design and you want to avoid that "peas in a pod" look.

If, however, you plan to use a strong, definite color for a front door, keep in mind that sometimes that door will be standing open. It should harmonize with the scheme of the room into which it opens, whether entry hall or living room, so that it seems a part of that room also.

There are those old "trompe l'oeil" effects for exterior painting, also. Chimneys that are out of proportion to the house, either too large or too small and weak-looking, will blend better if they are painted the same color as the house.

If a roof-line is cut up with too many gables, draw the eye down by featuring the front door or shutters, keeping paint on the roof-line inconspicuous.

A house with a jumbled look from too many window and door openings of odd sizes and shapes will look better with trim the same color as the house itself. Accenting the trim by a different color will only call attention to the defects. Perhaps it would also be a good idea in this case to remove some of the shutters on all the small windows, leaving them only on the larger, more uniformly-sized ones.

13

A house painted a lighter color will appear larger than one painted in a darker shade. A contrast in color between siding and trim, siding and brick or stonework, etc., will draw the eye for a more striking effect.

The various paint companies have made it easy for us with their traditional lines of exterior paint colors that have been researched and are authentic colors as they appeared in historic Williamsburg, Savannah, Charleston, New Orleans, and Cape Cod, to name a few.

Transparent and opaque wood stains afford us many possibilities both traditional and modern. It is even possible to have, with an applied bleach treatment, the lovely weatherbeaten color of driftwood, previously only possible in a house by the sea.

It is only recently in this country of white frame houses that color has been confidently used on the outside. There is no reason why we cannot brighten our exteriors. An Early-American salt-box house takes on a striking aspect painted in curry yellow with white trim and a black door. A Victorian house could be exciting in eggplant with white painted gingerbread trim. With all the paints and gradations of color available for the exterior now, the sky's the limit for new and bright ideas!

Practical Hints

- *In making decisions on color, it is important to keep in mind the fact that the finished job will look darker than the sample, particularly if paint is being used on a large area.*
- *Look at color samples in the same light as the conditions under which they will be used—natural light for exterior, filament or fluourescent lighting for interior.*
- *The size of the area in many cases will affect the values of color. Wall areas that reflect each other will intensify and purify each other's color, tending to removal of gray tones.*
- *When you check color samples against other colors in a room, remember also to check against the colors which will be visible when the doors to adjoining areas are standing open. Smooth color transitions from room to room are important in achieving complete color harmony.*

Now that you have decided on your color scheme, either for interior or exterior, you are ready to proceed to shop for paint. The chapters to come will give you advice on choosing paint, on preparing the surface and on application, so that you can avoid the mistakes which cost so many people time and money.

14

2
Success by Avoiding Failure

Any one of 17 signs on a painted surface point to trouble that you can identify and correct. It's much easier to spend a few minutes assuring success than to have to repaint an entire job because you didn't. After listing these signs and describing preventive measures, we will, later in the chapter, do the same for troubles unique to certain kinds of surfaces. We will, finally, identify troubles caused by faulty structural design.

Here are the 17 signs that apply to all surfaces:

Chalking. A light, chalky dust often forms on weathered exterior paints. The general theory to explain it is that sunlight on titanium dioxide causes a chemical and physical deterioration of the resin or oil in the paint. Some forms of titanium dioxide actually are included in a formulation because they cause chalking, the notion being that this chalk is washed off by rain, taking dirt along with it.

Old paints probably chalk because they're old and need replacing. When such chalks are excessive, they may cause repainting difficulties; hence, they must be removed as thoroughly as possible. Primers used over them must contain sufficient oil or additive to aid adhesion by thoroughly wetting any invisible chalk that may remain after cleaning.

Blistering. These bloated areas on a painted surface usually result from one of two conditions: one occurs when moisture is absorbed by water-sensitive components of poor paint and then builds up enough pressure to cause swelling. The other kind of blister forms when trapped solvent tries to escape.

The remedy is to remove the blister and repaint the area, this time using high quality paints that are low in water-sensitive salts. If trapped solvent is to blame, make certain you don't repeat the cause—which was applying a second coat before the first coat was dry.

15

Fig. 2.1 Chalking on Residential Structure
Chalk from the painted wood shingles has washed down on the brick. Excess pigment in the paint is one of the most likely causes.

You may find a bare or semi-bare area in a painted surface, somewhat round in shape. This is probably the remains of a blister that popped under its internal pressure.

Flaking. Paint sometimes flakes off because foreign matter—dust or grease—on the surface at the time of painting may have interfered with adhesion; or an old coat of paint left on the surface may have lost adhesion, taking new coats with it. When flaking occurs, trouble with succeeding coats can be avoided by sanding down the flaked area, allowing only sound old paint to remain. A moderate amount of sanding should remove all but the sound paint.

Flaking on wood surfaces often is caused by inadequate calking where wood meets metal or a cement surface. Water seeps into the wood, causing it to swell. Paint separates and flakes off.

Correct this by scraping off all calk at joints near the flaking and re-calk before repainting. (See Chap. 3.)

Peeling. Small sheet-like areas may peel from concrete porches and steps, bricks, and galvanized metal. Porches and steps in contact with the ground, either directly or through concrete foundations, often are affected by ground water, which rises by a wicking action through somewhat porous concrete. Porch and step paints are usually tough and impermeable to water; hence, pressure is built up behind these paints when ground water passes up. With nowhere to go, the pressured water

This elegant fireplace wall was created by panels framed with wood moulding, painted to simulate Colonial paneling in this remodeled living room. (Western Wood Moulding Photo)

This pleasant living room illustrates the use of traditional paint colors (Williamsburg Blue) in the traditional way by accenting the fireplace, moulding, wainscoting, and windows. This treatment can be very fresh and appealing. (Interior Design, E. Gordon Findley, ASID, and Douglas B. Kohler, ASID; Hedrich-Blessing Photo)

In this room setting a Picasso print started the whole color scheme. The red-orange of the horseman was picked up on the large chair and darkened for the carpet and table skirt. The brown, black and white fabric repeats the charcoal of the print and adds interest. (Hercules, Inc.)

(Top right) Fabric on a screen is the source for the color scheme here, ranging from the soft gold in the damask fabric to the bright green of the walls. (Hercules, Inc.)

Blue-green and red-orange in a complementary color scheme at its most dramatic! The graphic design created by the carpet and painted strips draws the eye to the seating arrangement. (Hercules, Inc.)

A good example of an analogous color scheme using yellows and oranges that are next to each other on the color wheel. Notice the use of black and white accents. This studio apartment succeeds in being warm and gay. (Hercules, Inc.)

In this inviting room, white was used to mask out an unattractive fireplace and adjoining windows. Dark, mellow wood accents the ceiling beams and floor. The white walls, of course, are an ideal background for the collection of paintings. (Marion Heuer, ASID; Hedrich-Blessing Photo)

Gay, bright graphics painted on the wall give this recreation room its carnival feeling and personality. (The Carpet and Rug Institute)

This light and lively Florida room gets its spirit from the side-by-side color scheme of yellow, yellow-green and green. The white painted rattan furniture adds the crispness that gives this room sparkle. (The Carpet and Rug Institute)

(Opposite page) A fine example of color coordination throughout the house. Note how the basic color complementary scheme is carried from room to room, with first the blue-green and then the red-orange as the dominant color. (Photographed at Wood Creek Courts, Lincolnshire, Ill.; Hedrich-Blessing Photo)

A sophisticated bathroom in blue and gold. Notice how the gold is used over all the walls, trim, doors and cabinets to add to the effect of dramatic simplicity. (Architect, G. Hugh Tsuruoka; Builder, Kepler and Clark; Hedrich-Blessing Photo)

Unusual ceiling treatment accented in green and white provides architectural interest in this attractive kitchen. Note how the different treatment and color of the cabinet doors adds to this effect. (Hedrich-Blessing Photo; A St. Charles Kitchen)

A fine backdrop for a collection of blue and white pottery in this family room with its warm beige walls and rich wood. (Interior Design, Mary Jane Graham, ASID; Hedrich-Blessing Photo)

A happy balance in this living room between serene, cool blue and warm, cheerful golden yellow. Notice how the white chair rail ties the print of the draperies and the sofa together, while adding architectural interest to the room. (Designed by Karl Steinhauser, ASID, for Futorian Furniture; Hedrich-Blessing Photo)

A striking Triad color scheme of red, blue, and yellow. Black and white are effective accents to help to achieve balance. A very exciting room. (Designed by Hans Juergens; Hedrich-Blessing Photo)

White walls used here as background for the grouping of brightly-colored posters and prints. (Interior Design, Sherl Coleman, ASID; Hedrich-Blessing Photo)

Here is a fine example of creating an illusion with paint. The orange and black headboard and canopy are simulated with the use of paint and wood moulding. (Architect, Irving Moses & Associates; Decorator, Barry Brukoff; Hedrich-Blessing Photo)

A bright bedroom in a monochromatic color scheme. The white painted furniture contributes a light and effective accent. (The Carpet and Rug Institute)

Barn red on neat and trim clapboard siding with white trim and slate blue door and shutters . . . a pleasing combination with the fieldstone wall. Notice that shutters were left off the oddly-placed windows and on the two larger windows where they not only would have looked out of place but have been obviously non-functional as well. (Hedrich-Blessing Photo)

Barn red again, but this time on rough-textured siding with white trim, door, and shutters with cedar shakes and mellow brick. Everyone's favorite! (Courtesy, Dexter Door Hardware; Hedrich-Blessing Photo)

This attractive two-toned color scheme gives this traditional house a distinctive appearance. But perhaps you are contemplating a change? The page opposite shows how, with simple sketches, you can test new ideas and visualize different color schemes on your own house. It's fun to try out several different ideas before reaching the final decision. (Ralph D. Huszagh, Architect, for John S. Clark and Sons; Hedrich-Blessing Photo)

Color wheel from The Oxford Companion to Art, edited by Harold Osborn, 1970, by permission of the Clarendon Press, Oxford. Drawings on Page 23 refer to the colors as shown.

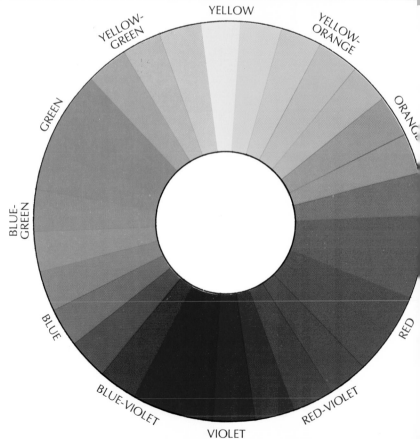

YELLOW

YELLOW-GREEN

YELLOW-ORANGE

GREEN

ORANGE

BLUE-GREEN

RED

BLUE

RED-VIOLET

BLUE-VIOLET

VIOLET

A medium blue–gray on the siding with a slightly lighter tone of the same color on the trim and a bright and welcoming red door gives the same house a different appearance.

Lemon yellow with white trim and a shiny black door gives the house a pretty bright look. It also appears larger. Note that the chimney has been painted white for a lighter effect. The accent has been put on the first floor windows only, while the second floor window is painted the same color as the wall.

In this example the siding has been finished with an opaque wood stain, while the window trim is white—a very neat look! The front door is also finished in a lighter wood stain. Notice that in all three illustrations the garage doors have not been accented.

(Top, left) Come right in and make yourself comfortable, says this Dutch-Colonial entrance! The cheerful yellow walls with white shutters at the windows as well as the colorful painted design on the door help to achieve this happy feeling. (Courtesy Dexter Door Hardware; Hedrich-Blessing Photo)

(Top, right) A stately doorway indeed! The Colonial woodwork surrounding the doors is accented in white against the gray-beige of the siding and doors. (Courtesy Pease Ever-Strait Door Co.; Hedrich-Blessing Photo)

Yellow daisies are a cheerful sight by this doorway. The shiny black door is an effective contrast to the translucent gray-green wood stain of the house. (Hedrich-Blessing Photo)

Fig. 2.2 Blistering. Large blisters formed and broke under this eave. Cause was moisture reaching the crawl space above the eave, below the sloping roof.

Fig. 2.2a Improper Coating Application Likely to Lead to Blistering. An open invitation to trouble. Blisters will probably form because an oil paint is being applied over condensed moisture, thereby lessening adhesive forces.

Fig. 2.3 Flaking. Incompatible topcoat lifted off this wood after a few months. Primer and topcoat came from different manufacturers.

29

works against the paint and causes it to lose adhesion.

The best way to overcome this problem is to lay drains to interrupt the flow of ground water before it reaches the foundation. If this is impractical, use a latex paint, which will let the water pass through without harming the paint. This, however, usually means sacrificing durability, because these paints are less tough than the usual porch and step paint.

Peeling on bricks may also come from ground water, or because water in the newly laid mortar between bricks did not dry before paint was applied, and the water may have migrated to the brick's face, causing loss of adhesion.

Bricks may suffer from a condition called efflorescence, which also may lead to peeling. Efflorescence results when salts in the brick are deposited on the face by water passing through. If the paint is permeable, the water takes the salts with it and deposits them on the paint's surface. Otherwise, the salts and the water press up behind the paint barrier. Even when the water is reabsorbed by the brick, which happens, the salts remain, seeded out behind the paint, causing it to lose adhesion.

When these efflorescing salts appear on unpainted brick, they should be carefully removed before painting.

Peeling brick may also result from a bad habit of bricklayers who remove flecks and dabs of dried mortar with muriatic acid (dilute hydrochloric acid). If not washed off thoroughly, the acid produces chloride salts on the surface. These are able to absorb water from latex paints, making them swell and leading to peeling.

If no other cause can be assigned to the peeling of bricks, then assume that muriatic acid is responsible. Wirebrush until only sound paint remains and then repaint. If the surface was painted recently and it peels, assume it was affected by muriatic acid. Remove the entire peeling area, and neutralize the muriatic acid with an alkaline bath consisting of trisodium phosphate, obtainable at any paint store. Be certain to rinse it off thoroughly.

Galvanized metal. May peel because chemicals deposited on the treated surface after the galvanizing bath may not have been properly removed. Galvanized metal should weather at least six months to eliminate these chemicals prior to painting. If you must paint before that time, ask your source to recommend a pre-painting treatment for the particular product you have. Do the same if a painted surface peels. Remove the paint and treat as the supplier recommends before repainting.

Selection of paint for galvanized metals demands care. (See Chapter 6.)

Lifting of Coats. Coats of paint may separate from each other or from the base because primer and topcoat are incompatible or because of faulty application of the topcoat.

Fig. 2.4 Deterioration on Galvanized Steel Gutter. This galvanized steel gutter was painted before adequate weathering could remove processing chemicals, and peeling resulted.

Sometimes the topcoat won't adhere to the primer; and if the wrong topcoat is used, it may have such strong solvents that it dissolves some of the primer, thus weakening the latter's hold on the surface, causing both paint films to lift.

Application of the topcoat before the undercoat has dried thoroughly can also cause lifting.

A topcoat may "crawl" if it is applied to the wrong undercoat. This is what usually happens if a latex paint is applied over a high-gloss enamel that hasn't been scuffed up enough to provide a perch for the paint.

Coats that lifted or "crawled" should be removed. Repainting should be in accordance with directions in Chapter 5.

Cracking. Most cracks in paint result from old age and inability to expand and contract at the same rate as the surfaces they cover. Several kinds of cracks may be seen: *checks,* or fine cracks in the topcoat; *crazing,* which is deeper and broader; and alligatoring, a severe form of crazing resembling an alligator hide. (Occasionally cracking is caused by depositing too much paint on the surface.)

Floating and flooding. A mottled, splotchy surface caused by separation of the components of a blended color, such as the yellow and blue that make green, is called *floating.* When one of the separated colors dominates and provides a uniform but unwanted color, this is known as *flooding.* The only remedy is to rough up the surface, if the paint is sound, and repaint—using a high quality paint this time. Floating and flooding are sure signs of a poorly formulated paint.

Wrinkling. Application of excess paint can lead to wrinkling. The best safeguard here is to spread paint uniformly and just enough to hide the surface thoroughly. Too heavy a topcoat makes it difficult for the undercoat

31

to dry completely. This undercoat, although sufficiently hard to be topcoated, nonetheless may take several days for through-dry. A heavy topcoat will almost certainly cause the undercoat to dry at a substantially slower rate than the over-coat. Tensions are set up between the two because the undercoat is still trying to yield its solvent, or water, after the topcoat is hard and dry. Wrinkling develops as the undercoat gradually dries.

Avoid this by applying both coats at the proper thickness.

Wrinkling and Faulty Stirring. Improper stirring of solvent-reduced paints causes different rates of drying. These paints dry by combining with oxygen in the air, a reaction aided by certain metal salts known as *driers,* or catalysts. Uneven distribution causes uneven drying rates; and the resultant tension leads to wrinkling. Poorly made, cheap paints may have too much drier and this, too, can lead to wrinkling. Play safe and thoroughly stir the high quality paints to which you should limit yourself.

Stringiness. A stringy coating is one that has started drying so rapidly that it doesn't have time to flow out and level. Even a cheap, cut-rate bargain store paint that does this should be returned and a different product bought, even if it costs more.

Ugliness is just one reason to avoid stringy paint. Poor adhesion is another. The coating dries so fast it can't penetrate either a fresh surface or an undercoat. So when stringy paint is seen, halt. Let it dry, remove it, and get a quality paint.

Brushmarks. Clear brushmarks on the surface, just like stringiness, result from overly rapid drying. Poor formulation may be to blame, but not always. Sometimes a properly formulated paint may have been used over a porous surface or an undercoat that is porous enough to draw solvent or water from the freshly applied topcoat.

When the water, or solvent, is rapidly drawn into the porous material, the topcoat loses its fluidity, thickens and dries so rapidly that the brushmarks don't have time to level out.

Avoid brushmarks in high quality paints by sealing porous surfaces properly (see Chapt. 3.) and by making certain that undercoats are not porous, which is another way of saying that their quality should match that of the high grade topcoats that you should be committed to buying.

Orange peel. These small depressions in the surface of sprayed paint may happen because the painter cuts paint intended for brush or roller application, using a solvent that evaporates too rapidly when sprayed.

To avoid this, buy paint with instructions on the can for spray application. Guessing what solvent to add may lead to orange peel, or even *sags* and *runs,* if addition of too much solvent or the wrong solvent makes the paint too thin.

32 *Stippling.* When rollers are used instead of brushes, some limited, almost

invisible fuzziness almost always appears. If the coating dries too fast, the fuzziness becomes so pronounced that it resembles stippling. You can usually anticipate stippling if the roller tends to drag, which is a sign that the paint is setting up before it even leaves the roller.

Avoid this trouble by taking the product back when you notice dragging and ask the dealer for a higher-quality product.

Sheen Variations. Faulty formulating may cause satin and semigloss films to flow out unevenly, leading to variations in the sheen of the surface. Another cause may be the use of an unsuitable primer when semigloss or full gloss topcoats are used.

For this reason, the use of recommended primers is especially important for gloss (or enamel) systems.

Primers for these coatings are specially formulated to have "enamel holdout," or the ability to resist any resin or solvent from the freshly applied enamel topcoat. These glossy topcoats are, by nature, loaded with resin and solvent, so they have a tendency to yield some of this material to already-dried primers if the latter have any degree of porosity.

Since the porosity of the primer may vary along the surface, the amounts of resin or solvent lost by the topcoat may vary, causing inconsistent ratios of resin to pigment in the enamel topcoat. Gloss depends on having a lot of resin. Consequently, gloss or sheen is diminished to the extent that resin is lost.

Similar inconsistencies in gloss occur when primer is applied too thinly. Then, if the surface is porous (like plaster or wallboard), resin from the enamel topcoat may pass through the skimpy primer and be absorbed by the porous surface.

Loss-of-gloss. When virtually the entire primer, or surface below, is absorbing resin somewhat uniformly from the enamel and the supposedly glossy surface has become dull, this is known as loss-of-gloss.

Sheen variations and loss-of-gloss can be avoided by using gloss and semigloss enamels that are made by reputable manufacturers and by following their recommendations for primers.

Skin on Surfaces. When a hard skin-layer forms on a painted surface and a soft, incompletely-dried layer is underneath, we probably have a poorly formulated solvent-thinned paint.

Sometimes skin forms because painting was carried out in a high wind. This accelerates drying of the surface. The under portion has its solvent trapped beneath the hardened top and, to make it worse, oxygen that is needed for drying is choked off.

Don't try to paint over skinned paint. Remove the old coat and repaint.

Excess Paint on Surface. Sagging, a condition in which the surface seems like a frozen cascade, is caused by depositing too much paint, particularly when it is on a sharp incline or if the paint is formulated to flow very easily. The excess paint flows off the brush down the surface. Unless brushed out quickly by the painter, it tends to "freeze" as it dries.

Other results of excess paint on the surface are *cracking* as a consequence of tensions developing between the top drying portions and the interior, whose rate of dry is inhibited by the heavy deposit above it; *wrinkling,* which has the same cause, except that the interior dries first; and *blistering,* which results when solvent trapped below tries to escape through the dried surface.

These conditions should be corrected by sanding smooth and repainting.

Avoid excess paint buildup by following the recommendations of the manufacturer for rate of spread, which usually is geared to adequate hiding of the surface below.

Dirt. Scrub off dirt with detergent and a brush or rag, but make certain that the "dirt" is not actually mildew.

Mildew. If mildew is suspected, rub the stained surface with a rag bearing detergent and diluted household bleach. Mildew appears greyish-green and will yield more easily than dirt, seeming to smear rather than spread.

Before repainting, remove mildew thoroughly. (See Chapter 3 for details.) Otherwise, the new coating will soon be contaminated, even if it has been adequately fortified with mildewcide.

Troubles Unique to Specific Types of Surfaces. The 17 general signs of trouble cited above are only part of the story. Each of the three types of surface—cement, metal, and wood—has its own unique problems that should be recognized and corrected.

*Cement Surfaces.** Poorly formulated mortar mixes often cause poor paint performance.

Popping. An eruption of soft, crumbly popouts may develop in concrete, stucco, or plaster. This is usually the result of varying degrees of porosity caused by poorly mixed, or inadequately cured, or improperly formulated material. When water reaches this porous, badly prepared material, some areas soften, others swell and pop. Holding paint on this is impossible.

This condition can be anticipated if you note an uneven gloss on these surfaces when they have been painted. This means that the porousness of the cement surface (always inconsistent) has caused irregular absorption of the resin in the paint, which varies the reflectivity, or degree of gloss, of the coating.

The remedy for popping is to remove the unsound material and

---

*The term "cement" is used throughout this book to cover materials involving cement, such as concrete, brick, cinder and concrete block, and wallboard—those materials normally covered by the technical term "cementitious," an unfamiliar word.

Fig. 2.5 Mildew. Hot shower steam provided an ideal environment for mildew.

patch with new mortar, allowing enough time for proper aging. (See Chap. 3 for surface preparation of cement material.) Sound cement on the surface, although porous, can be saved by coating with a primer-sealer and then topcoating with a paint with low permeability and low water absorption (See Chap. 6.). Care must be taken, in all instances, that the cause of moisture, usually improper calking or sealing, is eliminated. (See Chap. 3.). If ground water is entering the structure and causing popping, the source of ground water must be eliminated.

Powdery deposit (efflorescence). An excess of soluble salts in a cement mix may be picked up by water diffused through the dried product. The water-borne salts may also pass through the coating and be deposited on its surface as a light powder. However, when the coating won't let the water pass, the salts work their way behind the paint and cause spotty loss of adhesion, and lifting. The treatment for this condition is described in Chap. 3.

Paint-Concrete Crumbling. If wet concrete is painted, contraction of the drying paint lifts it and sometimes draws the still-wet cement with it.

When other causes are ruled out and this cause is probable, remove the crumbled surface and replace with patching compound, allowing the recommended time for curing.

Metal Surfaces. Unlike potentially porous material like concrete, metal can't feed moisture to a coating by wicking action, nor does it normally expand and contract like wood.

So metal rarely sins against paint; it usually is sinned against by faulty preparation, wrong paint selection, or abuse—either from individuals or by brute weather.

Steel and iron. Rust is the payoff for abuse of steel or iron—no matter the cause. With rust on a surface that is to be painted or repainted, you can be certain the protective film will fail before long.

Treating rust. First, it is necessary to determine the cause. If a dent   35 or chip is responsible, this indicates that nothing fundamental is wrong. If such dents are likely to continue to occur, use of a paint with greater impact resistance may be necessary. (See Chap. 6.)

Determine if the rusty area is near the metal's edge. If so, possibly the edge wasn't painted. So paint it, after first sanding or wire-brushing the edge and the rusty portion.

Note if the metal is very thin and if rust appears at a point where flexing occurred. That probably indicates the paint isn't flexible enough and ruptured. Find a flexible paint (See Chap. 6.).

And finally, if none of these causes is apparent, the metal may be rusting because it was improperly cleaned prior to painting. Or, a surface blemish born in the forge or at the rolling mill may be to blame. This is called *mill scale,* a form of oxidation, wavy and multicolored, that results from high temperature when the metal is formed.

When mill scale is responsible, and it is recognized after paint removal, it must be taken off.

Rust or mill scale must be completely removed before painting. Paint immediately after rust removal, because invisible amounts of trouble-making oxidants form and start the rust process as soon as even modest amounts of moisture are present in the atmosphere.

Aluminum, tin, copper, or brass. These materials are often unpainted, but when paint has been applied for some reason, it may fail because of improper cleaning or pretreatment. (See Chapter 3 for information about pretreatment and suitable coatings.)

Wood. Major causes of trouble in painted wood result from the nature of wood itself. Its chemical content under some circumstances can cause staining on a paint's surface; and because much lumber is composed of alternate areas of hard and soft layers, or rings, stresses are set up when moisture penetrates it or the weather changes. These stresses cause poorly formulated paints to lose their adhesion.

Discoloration from natural wood chemicals. Redwood and cedar contain natural soluble dyes that may be diffused by moisture reaching, in one way or another, to the wood's surface. Dyes are dissolved and pass through the paint, forming pink or brown streaks on its surface.

Prevent this by using a good sealer, either a specially formulated one or white shellac. Do not use a porous latex paint on these woods. White lead pigment in linseed oil or alkyd resin formerly took care of this situation, but federal regulations now ban lead pigments in or near households. New substitute paints are available. You will have to depend on your dealer. Read the label carefully. (See Chapter 6 for the kind of paint to request.)

Trouble due to stresses. Most hard woods have two kinds of growth: spring growth, which is fast and soft and covers a relatively wide span in the trunk, and summer growth, which is slower, harder and in a more narrow band.

The soft woods absorb more moisture than harder summer wood, so they swell at a different rate, causing stress in the coating that protects the surface. Trouble mostly appears when you are using wood that is cut with the grain, which can be recognized by wide, irregular waves of alternating hard and soft bands. In wood that is cut across the grain, the pattern is tighter and the difference in swelling is minimized.

Flat-patterned wood is more decorative and is desirable for woodwork and furniture, but should be avoided for construction.

If you must paint a flat-patterned wood for some reason, then select paints with outstanding adhesion and flexibility.

Green lumber. Some paint failure is due to use of green wood, which usually contains considerable natural water. Kiln-drying should have removed this. If paint fails on green wood, remove it and hope that by the time it is repainted the wood will have seasoned naturally.

Plywood problems. Plywood, which is peeled from logs, has the same sort of stresses found in flat-patterned wood. Moisture enters the plies and triggers the unresolved stresses, which loosen the paint, causing peeling or cracking.

Plywood that is likely to be exposed to moisture should be sealed before painting with a water repellent.

Another precaution for plywood, particularly poor grades that may be laminated by inferior adhesives, is to make certain that the edges of the plies are protected by a sealer plus some of the topcoat selected for the face. This holds off moisture, so the adhesive won't be penetrated and loosened.

Troubles due to failure by design. Now, you know, of course, that this title doesn't mean that builders deliberately design structures so that paint fails.

The phrase "failure by design" connotes that faulty design, or indifferent construction, assures continued failure of paints on the affected surfaces. Hence you as a resident should recognize and correct these faults.

Since this is such an important facet of successful painting, we are turning to a study carried out for the Armed Forces with the cooperation of the National Bureau of Standards and will cite it generously, and almost word for word:

Moisture, the major cause of abnormal deterioration of coatings, may come either from external sources or may be developed within the structure. Abnormal deterioration of applied coatings in essentially porous materials can result from the passage of water to inside walls. If the walls are wet and the outside surface is warmed, as by sunlight, the

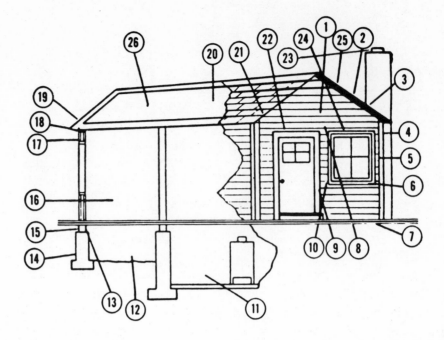

Fig. 2.6 Moisture from within Structure. Twenty-six points of potential moisture trouble in a poorly built house: (1) built with green lumber; (2) no cricket or saddle where chimney meets roof: (3) no flashing at side of chimney; (4) use of metal corner caps; (5) exposed nail heads not galvanized; (6) no window sash at sill; (7) wood contacts earth; (8) no drip or gutter at eaves; (9) poorly fitted window and door trims; (10) waterproof paper not installed behind trim; (11) damp, wet cellar unventilated at opposite sides; (12) no ventilation of unexcavated space; (13) no blocking between unexcavated space and stud wall space; (14) no waterproofing or drainage tile around cellar walls; (15) lacks foundation water and termite sill; (16) plaster not dry enough to paint; (17) sheathing paper should be waterproof but not vapor proof; (18) vapor barrier omitted—needed for present or future insulation; (19) built during wet, rainy season without taking due precaution or ventilating on dry days; (20) built hurriedly of cheap materials; (21) inadequate flashing at breaks, corners, roof; (22) poorly jointed and matched; (23) no chimney cap; (24) no flashing over openings; (25) full of openings, loosely built; (26) no ventilation of attic space.

moisture will tend to move to the outside atmosphere. However, if nonpermeable coatings are used, (most paints other than latex or cement paints), this moisture will be trapped and will build pressure until eventually it will cause the coating either to blister or lose adhesion. The multitude of ways moisture can give trouble in a poorly built house are shown in Fig. 2.6.

Moisture from within the structure. A major cause of excessive moisture is that developed in normal use by the occupants of the structure. These are the sources of such moisture per day:

Breathing and perspiration	2 lbs.
Cooking and dishwashing	1 lb.
Clothes washing and drying	8 lbs.
Showers—daily	1/2 lb.

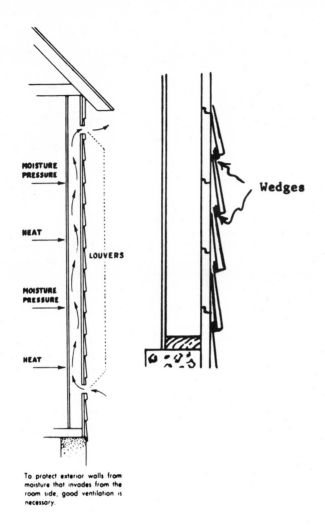

MOISTURE PRESSURE

HEAT

LOUVERS

MOISTURE PRESSURE

HEAT

Wedges

To protect exterior walls from moisture that invades from the room side, good ventilation is necessary.

Fig. 2.7 Venting of Outside Walls. Good venting of outside walls is necessary to protect the exterior coating from damage by moisture originating in the inside of the structure.

Fig. 2.7a Vents to Release Moisture. The round louvered vent is inserted in exterior wood walls to free trapped moisture after a hole is drilled to receive it. A long, barreled vent is inserted in thick concrete or brick walls.

The total is about 1-1/2 gals. of water per person per day without including moisture given off by heaters. So venting is required for all equipment, and kitchens and shower rooms should have exhaust fans in operation during use of facilities. Failure to have these can be ascribed to poor design.

Humidity. The humidity within a structure should be kept fairly low, especially during periods when outside walls are cold. Otherwise, moisture will collect and eventually work its way into and through the interior walls and on through the outside walls unless the interior paint on the

39

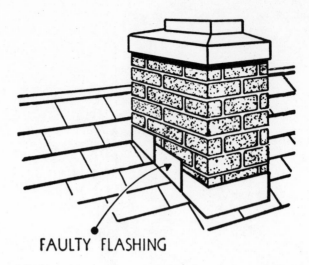

FAULTY FLASHING

Fig. 2.8 Metal flashing, improperly arranged, can cause moisture to enter house and seek to escape.

walls is impermeable. The following humidity levels should be the maximum within a structure for indoor air temperatures of 70 F.

Outside Temp. F		Inside Humidity (Max.) (percent)
Below	−20	15
−20 to	0	20
0−	20	30
Above	20	40

Most of the structural defects listed in the 26 Points to check lead to moisture trouble, many of them described earlier in the chapter under the heading of cracks, peeling, blisters, and obviously related to water and its unfortunate effect on paint.

Unless you are thoroughly familiar with your blueprints and can analyze your own trouble, it may be wise to call on a local contractor to see just which if any of these faults apply to your house.

Also remember that even if moisture-caused troubles are leading to failure, relatively simple steps described in Chapter 3 may be all you need. A thorough reading of the section on calks and sealants should also help show you how to stop most moisture problems.

3

First Prepare
the Surface

Just about anyone with reasonable muscle power can stroke paint onto a surface. Getting it to stay there, while not an intellectual accomplishment, does demand attention to a few details, which, simple as they are, most painters often overlook.

Most of the mistakes that ruin a paint job are made before a paint brush, or roller, even reaches a surface. No paint yet made can overcome the handicap of a surface that is dirty, greasy, wet, chalky, cracked, or unreceptive in general; and it must be said, the paint industry, or at least its best members, are making some truly remarkable paints, if you'll just use them correctly.

That's why you, as a painter or the purchaser of painting services, must know the kind and condition of the surface to be painted and how to make it receptive to the coating you decide to use.

Many a paint job has turned sour because the painter—professional or otherwise—ignored the few details needed for surface preparation, figuring that if you spend enough for a coating it'll stick, no matter.

That's like saying that if you buy Grade-A eggs you'll make a good omelette even if the frying pan is caked with charred crust.

Any responsible cook cleans up the surface of a pan before cooking or frying.

And, if you expect a successful paint job, the same holds true. What is certain is that you must prepare the surface.

Otherwise, forget it!! Sell your house and buy an all-plastic, antiseptic domicile and prepare to be bored to death by the year-in, year out monotony of unchanging colors.

If you want the vibrant freshness that a coat of paint brings to a room, or the sparkle that repainting the outside walls brings to your   41

Fig. 3.1 Handwork for Old Paint. A sharp scraper from your paint or hardware store combined with a little muscle can reduce blisters and flaking surfaces almost level. Sandpaper finishes the leveling process.

property, then follow a few simple rules, if you're doing the painting, or insist that your painter abide by them.

Six General Rules for Surface Preparation.

1. Clean off loose material, such as dust, rust, old paint, or anything that can be removed by hand, using a brush, broom, chisel, scraper, sandpaper, or steel wool.
2. Fill in holes and gouges, making certain they're smooth.
3. Clean off tight, stubborn material—grease, chemicals, gums, exudates—by using motorized equipment, such as power sanders or wire brushes.
4. If the surface is smooth and hard, or if a sound old coat of paint is present, some method of roughing is necessary to promote adhesion of the new coating. Simple sanding by hand or power sanding may be adequate, or mild chemicals may be needed to etch out an anchor pattern for the coating. Very rarely, for rock-hard concrete, a sandblasting firm may be required.
5. If the surface is inhospitable to the selected coating, chemical treatment may be needed to create a surface that is receptive.
6. Where two dissimilar materials, such as cement and wood, come together on an exterior surface, use a calking compound to cover any possible gaps that are almost certain to develop. If the joint is

likely to move to any extent, select a more flexible version of a calk, which is called a *sealant*.

The following paragraphs elaborate on the Six General Rules for Surface Preparation:

Hand cleaning. Simple hand cleaning includes the use of sandpaper, hand wirebrush, detergents, water, solvents, rags and brushes.

Modest sanding. New surfaces sanded lightly and followed by thorough brushoff, or detergent and water cleaning, should be ready for painting. The same preparation should be adequate for roughing and cleaning sound old coats of paint or removing loose paint.

Small areas. Hand cleaning may be preferable for small areas even when hard-to-stick coatings, such as epoxies and urethanes, are to be applied. These require a more thorough-going preparation than run-of-the-mill coatings, such as alkyds or oil paints. But why set up a mechanical device if only a small area is involved? Just sand a little harder, but with care that no gouging is done.

Holes and gouges. For most surfaces, small holes and gouges can be corrected with calking compound or spackle. Large holes, or cracks, however, may need a fabric bridge for repair. These materials consist of a thin web of fibreglass applied over a durable adhesive-paint and then topcoated with a special paint that makes the web disappear when applied properly.

Power cleaning. Equipment for power cleaning ranges from simple motor-driven wire brushes, sanding discs, or orbital flat sanders all the way to complicated needle guns and blasting machines hurtling natural sand and flint to prepare so-called anchor patterns on steel to make it receptive to epoxies or urethanes with relatively poor surface-wetting and penetrating ability. (The common paints, like alkyds, oils, latexes, phenolics, penetrate better.)

Wire brushes. These must be used carefully for two reasons. First, if over-used, they can erode the surface, often unevenly; second, excessive brushing can yield a polished surface, which will discourage adhesion. Light treatment provides desirable roughening.

Power sanders. As with hand-sanders, power driven versions must be used with paper suited to the job. (Details will be found in the section on preparing wood surfaces.)

Power blasting. Some power-driven blasters merely hurl water to remove large quantities of loose rust, or dirt; but the real heavy-weight blasting for such surfaces as rock-hard concrete is with abrasives, usually natural sand, or flint. Ground walnut shells or corn cobs are used for delicate surfaces.

Blasting is reserved for carefully-trained pros and may involve remov-   43 ing severe, tight rust, or mill scale. Tight rust and mill scale can cause coating failure on outdoor furniture, bicycles, or toys. When encountered on small areas, wire brush and repaint immediately. On large areas, get a professional.

Chemical treatment. Several types of chemical treatment are safe and harmless enough to be used by any reasonably cautious adult. These include alkali cleaning, using trisodium phosphate bought from a paint store; acid cleaning with mild phosphoric acid; paint removers, which require some care; and chemical surface modifiers, which put a new thin layer of surface over the inhospitable one, or may help improve corrosion resistance in an especially bad environment or if the painted object is to be used underwater.

Alkali-cleaning. Trisodium phosphate is consided safer than solvents for removing oil and grease. For stubborn contaminants, this alkali should be heated to about 150-200° F, the higher the better but below boiling. Never use any kind of alkali cleaner on aluminum or stainless steel.

Alkali cleaners should be thoroughly cleaned off with copious water rinses—preferably hot. Alkali allowed to remain on the surface may be worse than the original contaminants.

Acid-cleaning. Phosphoric acid, a relatively safe material, is used to clean iron and steel, and a weak solution of muriatic acid may be used to wash concrete that has any one of several signs of incompatibility with paint. (These signs and treatment will be fully covered later in this chapter in the section on preparing cement surfaces.)

Paint removers. These may be divided into two types: for easy to remove paints and heavy duty paint removers.

Various hydrocarbons and alcohols will remove oil, alkyd, and most latex paints. These include methyl alcohol and benzene. Some stronger proprietary materials are usually mixed with these to provide adequate strength.

Stronger removers are needed for epoxies, phenolics, vinyls, urethanes, factory-applied enamels, and other heavy-duty coatings. Most commonly used material is methylene chloride, which is somewhat toxic and must be handled carefully.

If these are limited because of environmental considerations, problems may follow, since other heavy-duty removers are based on rather exotic materials which should be used only by persons familiar with them. A knowledgeable paint store operator should be consulted about a safe product.

Chemical surface modifiers. When iron or steel surfaces will be constantly exposed to water, they should be modified to help prevent rust formation when the coating protecting them is chipped or worn away. Even scratches may allow rust to form and spread unless phosphates are used to treat the metal. These form iron phosphate, which discourages rust.

Getting Ready to Paint Cement Material

Watch out for the following: Construction defects that let moisture seep from behind or front; excess alkali in the cement mixture, which won't let the concrete, mortar, or spackle hold paint; shininess on the surface of concrete or stone, indicating it is so hard that paint can't penetrate the surface to enable it to adhere; fine, powdery chemicals on the surface of concrete, which either got there by floating to the surface when the concrete was setting or leached out after it cured; and newly-set poured or pre-cast concrete.

Each kind of trouble has its own solution.

Construction defects. Locate and correct them after checking chapter 2 which covers "Failure by Design." Any openings in the surface or connections with the ground should be sealed off to prevent wicking, whereby ground water rises in porous concrete or brick. Be generous in the use of calking compounds to seal off joints between dissimilar materials, such as concrete and wood.

Excess alkali. Freshly poured cement is alkaline until all the cement has had time to react with air to form carbonates, which are virtually neutral. Many contractors and builders are impatient to finish their jobs, so they don't wait the three months recommended for this weathering process before painting. As a result, paint often peels. Clean off the peeling paint and determine if the surface is still highly alkaline by testing with damp litmus paper. If excessively alkaline, use a mixture of phosphoric acid and zinc chloride to wash the surface thoroughly. Ask your paint dealer if the paint he sells is compatible with this mixture.

Shininess. If stone or concrete is very shiny prior to painting, or is found so after paint failure, it is probable that it is too hard for adhesion. In rock, this must be overcome by sandblasting. Dense concrete must be prepared by washing, followed by scrubbing with a 5 per cent solution, by weight, of muriatic acid, obtainable at any paint store. Try 10 percent if this doesn't work. Only allow the acid on the surface for five minutes. Longer will allow troublesome salts to form. Sponge or rinse off the acid as rapidly as possible. Don't work on more than four square feet at a time.

To see if the surface is ready to paint, place a few drops of water on it. Quick absorption means it's ready.

If this treatment doesn't work, two other steps may be tried. First, coat the surface with a solution of 3 percent zinc chloride and 2 percent

45

phosphoric acid and let it dry. This serves as a "tie-coat," which thus will not be influenced by the hardness of the cement. If that doesn't work, abrade the surface with a hard, rough stone.

Fine, powdery chemicals on the surface. Water passing through from the interior or through poorly-calked joints may pick up soluble salts and deposit them on the surface. The powdery residue is called *efflorescence.* When the powder results by floating to the surface during the curing process, it is called *laitance.*

No matter the name, brush or scrape it off. Then treat the surface with muriatic acid as described for shiny surfaces.

Newly-set poured or pre-cast concrete. Entrapped air in these types of concrete will eventually escape from their tiny pockets and rupture paint, thus letting water enter the concrete and further undermine the coating. Before painting these surfaces, sandblasting should be done by a professional.

Special types of cement surfaces.

Concrete block. Prepare by removing loose dust and dirt. If alkali or grease is present, remove by washing with a detergent and rinsing thoroughly. For appearance's sake and to prevent wastage of paint, use block fillers to seal and fill at least a good part of the voids. Low-priced materials are available, but fillers made of synthetic rubber are preferable. Use two coats if the voids are unusually large. Always allow at least 24 hours for the final coat to dry before applying paint.

Sprayed concrete. Although hard and dense, this material has few air pockets, and thus can be prepared by handcleaning unless the surface is very smooth, in which case try acid-etching before resorting to sandblasting. Use 1 part muriatic acid (30 percent), with 2 parts water, by volume. Apply 50–75 square feet per gallon. Rinse after two to three minutes.

Concrete floors. Smooth-troweled floors may not hold paint unless acid-etched or moderately sandblasted. Air pockets are not usually formed by troweling, so sandblasting, if used, need not be heavy.

Stucco. Since this consists of Portland cement mortar, sand, and perhaps coloring, it requires three-months weathering prior to painting to overcome usual alkalinity.

Plaster. Allow to dry at least one month before painting. Some roughening is needed if a high performance coating, such as an epoxy, urethane, or polyester is to be applied, and for these sanding should be right down to the plaster if old paint is present.

Spackling compound. Joints between sections of gypsum wallboard are usually covered with perforated tape and spackling compound, which consists of cement powder and a fibrous material, such as asbestos or talc. This material is also used for repairing small holes and cracks. Surfaces

46

to be spackled should be dampened. Use a putty knife or small trowel to fill the hole, allowing a little surplus on top to account for shrinkage. When thoroughly dry, sand smooth and paint like any other cement surface.

Patching plaster. For large holes in plaster, this is better than spackling compound, since it contains an accelerator to hasten hardening. Dampen the surface with clear water before applying. Arrange the plaster in a slight convex shape to allow for shrinkage, and sand smooth before painting.

Portland cement grout. Concrete and masonry cracks require Portland cement grout, which should be dampened for several days following repair.

Since most requirements will be small, buy this material, ready-made, from your hardware or paint store.

Bridging-Fabric. Bridging fabrics for problem cracks are available at most paint stores. They are particularly valuable wherever temperature changes are wide and expansion of the filler is likely to cause repetition of cracks. Kits are available, containing a flexible coating on which the fabric is placed, the fabric itself, and a flexible topcoat. Application is simple, and when done with moderate care, the fabric is invisible.

The system has proved particularly valuable where joints between chimneys and roofs have proven troublesome.

Getting Ready to Paint Wood Surfaces.

Watch out for the following: Excess moisture in wood, which should have been removed by kiln-drying; oil, grease and waxy contaminants that have penetrated the surface; knots and discolored sapwood; unsound wood (decayed or rotten); plywood with surface treatment and/or casein or animal glues binding the laminated plies; mildew; wood that requires filling; painted wood; joints with cement or metallic materials.

Overcoming troublemakers. The following methods should be helpful in overcoming the foregoing troublemakers.

Excess moisture. Don't buy wood unless assured it is adequately dried, which means its moisture content is as follows: for exterior woodwork—9–14 percent; for interior woodwork—5–10 percent; for wood flooring—6–9 percent. The lumber dealer should have a moisture meter to determine content.

Oil, grease or waxy contaminants. Clean the surface with a detergent or solvent, then seal the trapped material in the pores with a thin coat of aluminum paint, shellac, or knot sealer, as described in the following paragraph.

47

Knots or discolored wood. Many woods have sap or certain natural dyes that will be extracted by the solvent in paint applied over them, causing discoloration of the paint. Frequently, this will be concentrated around knots, leaving ugly blotches following the knot's outline. Where natural dyes or sap can be seen, with or without knots, apply a *knot-sealer paint,* or shellac, from your paint store. Old, discolored paint should be primed and topcoated. The alternative is to remove it and seal and topcoat.

Unsound wood (decayed or rotten). Unsound wood should be gouged out with a sharp instrument and replaced with plastic wood or putty.

Mildew. Even the suspicion of mildew on a surface to be painted makes it advisable to wash the surface with the following formulation, recommended by the National Paint and Coating Association:

2/3 cup trisodium phosphate
1/3 cup detergent powder
3   quarts warm water
1   quart ordinary household bleach

This makes a gallon. Use full strength. Scrub. Thoroughly rinse off.

Improperly glued plywood, or surface treated. Avoid this problem by buying American-made, high quality plywood. If you suspect surface treatment, clean off with steel wool followed with a mineral spirit rubdown. Paint remover may be faster. Surface treatment can cause adhesion trouble. If you're stuck with plywood held together by casein or animal glue (both water sensitive), protect the ends by coating them with a good water-based primer (water-based to increase the likelihood of compatibility with the glue). Follow with a second coat. Or, protect the ends with a water-based calk or sealant.

Wood that needs filling. An open-pore wood, listed in Table 3-1, requires a wood filler obtainable at any paint store. This consists of a fine silica in oil. Apply with a stiff brush and wipe off excess sealer with a dry rag—across the grain. Before priming, drive nail heads and screws beneath surface. Prime the surface, then use putty or plastic wood to fill holes. Sand uneven spots and paint.

Window sills or frames often have exposed ends with growth rings showing. These are porous and should be coated with a heavy primer-sealer to prevent absorption. Ends of wood going into masonry should also be treated this way.

Painted wood. Rough up a sound coat before repainting to aid adhesion. Loose paint must be removed by wire brushing or sand paper, taking care that brushing is limited. Stubborn paint on soft wood may be flame-cleaned, but only by a professional. Use paint removers on hard wood, and on soft wood if care is taken. (See page 106)

Table 3.1 Wood Classification According to Openness of Pores.

Name of Wood	Soft Wood	Hard Wood	Open Pore	Closed Pore	Notes
Ash		x	x		Needs filler
Alder	x			x	Stains well
Aspen		x		x	Paints well
Basswood		x		x	Paints well
Beech		x		x	Varnishes well, paints poorly
Birch		x		x	Paints and varnishes well
Cedar	x			x	Paints and varnishes well
Cherry		x		x	Varnishes well
Chestnut		x	x		Requires filler, paints poorly
Cottonwood		x		x	Paints well
Cypress		x		x	Paints and varnishes well
Elm		x	x		Requires filler, paints poorly
Fir	x			x	Paints poorly
Gum		x		x	Varnishes well
Hemlock	x			x	Paints fairly well
Hickory		x	x		Needs filler
Mahogany		x	x		Needs filler
Maple		x		x	Varnishes well
Oak		x	x		Needs filler
Pine	x			x	Variable
Teak		x	x		Needs filler
Walnut		x	x		Needs filler
Redwood	x				Paints well

Joints with cement material or metal. Sealants or calking compound must be used to stop entry of water at areas where wood meets other materials. Sealants are used where some movement is likely at the juncture. If wood is to be placed in concrete or stucco, use a primer sealer at the ends.

Getting Ready to Paint Metal.

Watch out for the following: a. Grease, dust or oil contaminants; b. Mill scale; c. Rust; d. Surfaces subject to heavy moisture; e. Galvanized steel and stainless steel; and f. Non-ferrous metals.

Grease, dust, or oil contaminants. Clean with detergents or by wiping with a cloth saturated with mineral spirits until all traces of contaminants have been removed. Rinse detergents; allow mineral spirits to evaporate.

Mill scale. This forms when steel is being processed and is a fore-runner

49

of some types of rust. Scale forms into three layers. The bottom layer is unstable and easily combines with oxygen and moisture from the atmosphere if uncoated or when coatings are broken. Rust results. The rust thus formed expands and loosens the top two layers, completely undermining paint on top.

Removal of mill scale. The first two methods for removal can be done by most handymen. First method is to use simple hand or powered tools to abrade it off, provided that alkyd, linseed oil or phenolic paints are used because of their ability to penetrate the minute amounts of rust and mill scale that are certain to remain. The second method requires an acetylene or some kind of blow torch to agitate the mill scale molecules and flake them off. Remember to paint while the surface is still hot; otherwise, rust may form immediately.

Two other methods, requiring professionals, are sandblasting and acid pickling, and should be considered when the surface is very large.

Rust. If such high performance coatings as epoxies, urethanes, or vinyl chlorides are to be used, rust must be completely eliminated, because unlike alkyds, linseed oil and phenolics these coatings cannot penetrate thin rust layers remaining after simple hand or powered cleaning.

Paints should always be applied as soon as possible after sanding, wirebrushing, or blasting, because moisture in the atmosphere can quickly start the rusting process.

Surfaces subject to heavy moisture. As soon as a painted surface is scratched, rust is likely to develop in a moist atmosphere.

Moisture with trapped oxygen works down to the metal surface through these cracks and forms rust, which spreads out under the coating unless a process called passivation is used.

Passivation. Even when rust forms at scratch points, the usual spreading beneath the paint can be avoided if metal is treated before painting with *passivators*, which actually change the composition of the metal surface. Hot or cold phosphates are used for this purpose.

Cold passivating uses phosphoric acid, about 5 to 7 percent by weight, with a wetting agent, and water dispersible solvent, and water. You can tell if the proper reaction has taken place if the material has dried to a greyish-white powder. If it's dark and sticky, the acid is too concentrated.

Galvanized steel, stainless steel and aluminum. These materials are difficult to paint without a pretreatment. To make them receptive to paint, they are coated with a very thin layer of a material known as a *wash primer.* This is a combination of phosphoric acid and zinc chromate in a resin known as polyvinyl butyral. This combination also acts, to some extent, as a passivator.

Aluminum, tin, copper, and brass. New materials should be solvent-cleaned to remove any thin protective coatings placed at the factory.

Fig. 3.2 Glazing Compounds. Windows and glass meet here, and friendly protection is needed against rain and wind. Glazing compounds are soft enough to fill the gaps between surfaces. Excess can be readily removed.

Before painting, a wash-primer of polyvinyl butyral and phosphoric acid should be used.

Calks and Sealants.

Calks and sealants are soft, moisture-repellent compounds that can be pressed into crevices, cracks or joints where one or more of the materials is porous. Calks are used for joints with very little or no movement. Sealants are mainly used for joints where some movement is anticipated.

The main function of calks and sealants is to seal the ends of porous materials so that water will not enter and cause trouble.

Failure to use calks or sealants leads to many surface failures that are blamed on paint. Porous surfaces, as has been noted repeatedly, may draw moisture to the surface where protective coatings may blister or become unsightly with salts or dyes drawn from below.

Ends of wood or cement materials must be calked or sealed prior to painting, unless priming is indicated. This simple step may end numerous unexplained paint failures.

51

Calks. These are simple compounds, consisting of a vegetable or fish oil or a synthetic binder, with a filler pigment to give it bulk and plasticity.

The binders do not dry hard right away. The interior actually remains soft during the calk's effective life, although the surface dries sufficiently to take paint.

Beware of junky, low-priced calks. If you see your painter using a no-name calk, ask him for details. Junk-calks may last one or two years if you're lucky. Then they may crack and let moisture enter the surfaces you're trying to protect.

It does not make sense to spend $600–800 or more for a paint job and then have it fail because the wrong calk was used.

And don't forget, if you're doing your own painting, your "sweat equity" in the job entitles you to know that you won't have to go through that again any sooner than necessary.

Don't settle for less than the best calk or sealant.

Suitable Calks. Butyl rubber and acrylic calks are recognized as the calks of choice.

Butyl rubber calk has a life expectancy of three to four years and costs little more than oil-based calks, which vary in life expectancy from one to four years, depending on your luck.

Acrylic latex calks offer life expectancy of at least five years, as tested, and should hold for 10 years.

Acrylic latex calks cost about 25–30 percent more than butyl calks and about twice as much as oil calks.

If you are careful about buying acrylic calks from reputable dealers who stand behind the brands they sell, you can expect the following advantages of acrylic latex calks, in addition to durability:

1. They are odorless, since they have no solvent.
2. They are easily worked into surfaces.
3. They can be applied to damp surfaces because they are latex.
4. They can be painted within 30 minutes of application.
5. They are more mildew resistant than oil types.
6. Calking knives, etc., can be cleaned with soap and water.

Precautions: Store these latex calks above freezing and apply them only when temperatures are above 40 F. And, be sure to remove any chalky deposits from surfaces and take off any old calks that may be present.

Sealants. The main characteristic distinguishing sealants from calks is *flexibility*. Joints where movement is likely require sealants. This includes movement due to vibration, shifting of joined surfaces, impact, and contraction and expansion due to swings in weather. Use sealants at those joints where elasticity is needed to maintain integrity of the seal.

Fig. 3.3 Calking. Calk between siding and window frame to avoid water leakage.

53

Fig. 3.4 Calking of Brick-Wood Interface. A brick-wood interface requires calking compound to prevent passage of moisture to rear of wood.

Sealants are of two basic types. The first type is based on *elastomeric* polymers, or stretchable resins, which set up and firm by the release of solvents stored in them. The second type is distinguished from the first because a chemical reaction must occur within the applied material before the product sets up and cures. These are known as chemical-curing compounds, and some of them reach the consumer in two parts and must be mixed and then placed in the applicator-gun. These two-packaged types are not recommended for use by any but experienced people. They will be described briefly for those who want to take the trouble to learn how to use them.

Elastomeric sealants. Sealants of this type are based on acrylics, butyl rubber, Neoprene, Hypalon. They are flexible and resist oil, chemicals, ozone, and heat, but they shrink to some extent and when elongated do not recover as well as the chemical curing sealants.

Acrylics with the flexibility needed for sealants are related to the type used for calks, but they are solvent-thinned rather than water-reducible. They have the advantage over most sealants in that they do not usually require priming. They have a wide choice of color and are self-sealing if torn by excessive movement.

Limitations of acrylics include strong odor, slow-cure, the heat needed for application, and their failure to withstand continuous water-immersion.

Butyl rubber. These are based on resins that are similar to that used for synthetic rubber tires. They are easy to work, low cost, easy to clean up, and are satisfactorily weather resistant. Life expectancy is 10–20 years, tack-free time 30 minutes to 6 hours.

Their limitations include inadequate recovery after stretching; probable shrinkage; less stretch and strength than other rubber sealants that cure chemically.

Neoprene®. A two-component version cures at room temperature, but the single package product needs heat. Neoprene sealants have a life expectancy of 30 years and dry to touch in less than four hours for two-component types, about four hours for the single. These sealants have good resistance to oil and gasoline and can stretch about 300 percent, but do not recover to that extent. Many also shrink and have poor color stability, but the two-component doesn't shrink.

Hypalon®. Has outstanding weather resistance. Some believe it will outlast just about any structure because it has excellent resistance to ozone, one of the worst atmospheric sources of damage.

Chemical-curing sealants. These are based on the following binders: polysulfides, polyurethanes, and silicones.

Polysulfides. These offer excellent elongation characteristics as well as recovery. They should last over 20 years.

It has been claimed that these will seal any joint, even if movement is expected to be 50 percent and the joints are wider than three-quarters of an inch.

Be sure to clean surfaces meticulously if these are to be used. If joints are wider than three-quarters of an inch, depth should be no more than one-half the width.

This is significant: you can use these for sealing joints involving marble, glass, white concrete, or plexiglas surfaces, provided that your dealer can get you a special *silane* primer.

Polyurethanes.   This is the most resistant of all sealers to deformation, which means it can be used on floors, even where lots of automotive traffic is expected. It also withstands considerable abrasion. Most surfaces don't need priming, but those, like glass, that do should have a silane primer. Some urethane sealants have the silane built into it. In any event, follow manufacturer's recommendations for priming.

Silicones.   These have the shortest tack-free time of all sealants, requiring only one hour or less if the humidity is right. Silicones adhere well to most surfaces, but the major manufacturer recommends priming all surfaces. Life expectancy is more than 20 years.

General Cautions about Calks and Sealants.   Use only dependable brands and the best available in the types selected.

Since two-component sealants are tricky to handle, read directions carefully. Many dealers may not be familiar with sealants, although they should be able to give dependable advice about calks.

The important thing about these two materials is an awareness of their importance, so you can judge the craftsmanship of your painter.

4
Ready, Set, Paint

A third phase of the painting operation, which often gets too little attention, is the setup of accessories and equipment.

Protecting innocent surfaces.

If possible move furniture, rugs and appliances away from walls where they interfere with movement of ladders. Drop cloths for above-ground exterior objects and either cloths or old newspapers for floors and rugs should provide ample protection.

Some professional painters put all moveable objects in the center of the room, moving them only when they are painting ceilings above this area. If everything is covered, the only need to move objects is to make way for ladders.

Painting exteriors requires drop cloths to protect shrubs, trees, and walks. Where shrubs come close to the house, drop cloths should be placed over the sides nearest the house, and, if necessary, rope should be used to tie back the vegetation until the surface has been painted and dried.

Shielding windows and trim.

If spray guns are to be used, masking tape should be placed on the area just beyond the surface to be sprayed. Effort required to mask, however, sometimes outweighs the advantage gained by spraying.

If brush or roller application is planned, simple flexible metal shields can be bought. Otherwise, a cardboard sheet such as those obtained *Ready, Set, Paint* with laundered shirts can be used to cover the edge beyond the area to be painted, whether it be moulding, trim, or window pane.

Ladders and Accessories.

An indispensable aid for most house painting, ladders also pose serious hazards. They should be selected carefully, with the user's limitations in mind.

Selecting a ladder. Types of ladders commonly used around a house are the stepladder and the extension ladder. An apartment dweller can handle his indoor jobs with a stepladder. A homeowner may also need an extension ladder for outdoor jobs.

Because of the danger caused by poorly designed ladders, standards have been established by the American National Standards Institute (ANSI), and the Underwriters' Laboratories, Inc. (UL). Play safe: buy only ladders bearing the seal of either of these organizations. If none is available, buy only branded ladders. In any event, check for weak steps or loose rungs, or metal hinges that function poorly. Take your time. Your neck is involved.

Is metal better than wood? Metal is lighter and will probably outlast wood. However, if you expect to work around electrical circuits, stick with wood.

New magnesium ladders now compete with aluminum. Weight of the ladder is about the same, but magnesium costs more and is likely to discolor.

Most expensive of all are metal ladders with fiber glass side rails, which are nonconductive, noncorrosive and more impact resistant than other ladders.

Stepladders. These are of three types: Type I, heavy duty (250 lbs. load-carrying); Type II, medium duty (225 lbs.); and Type III, light duty (200 lbs.). Steps should be flat and level when open. Distance between steps should be 12 inches or less. Depth of step should be at least 3-1/2 inches for wood and at least three-quarter inch thick. They should not protrude more than three-quarter of an inch beyond front of rail.

Don't buy a wood stepladder unless it has either a metal reinforcing rod or a metal angle brace. The bottom step should always have a metal angle brace. The reinforcing rod should have suitable metal washers at the ends to prevent damage to the side rails. Also at the center they should have wood or metal truss blocks separating them from the step.

Metal steps need only be three inches deep for 225 and 250 lb. capacity and 2-1/2 inches for 200 lb. capacity. They should be corrugat- 57

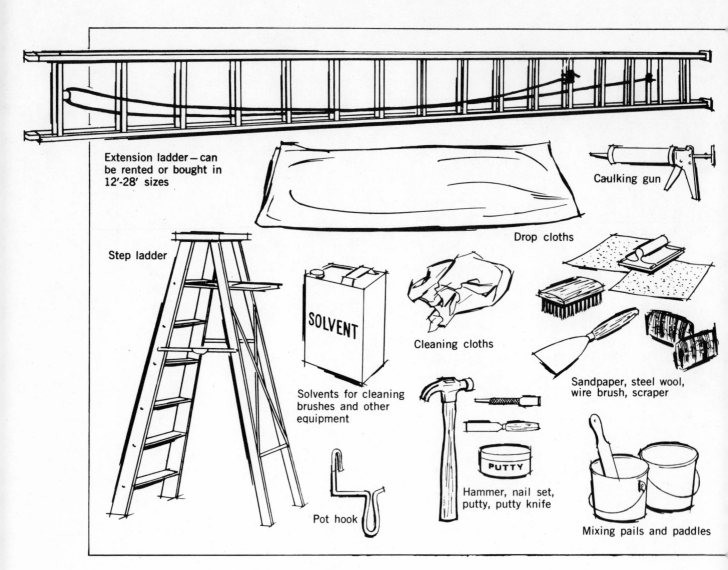

Extension ladder – can
be rented or bought in
12'-28' sizes

Caulking gun

Drop cloths

Step ladder

SOLVENT

Cleaning cloths

Solvents for cleaning
brushes and other
equipment

Sandpaper, steel wool,
wire brush, scraper

PUTTY

Hammer, nail set,
putty, putty knife

Pot hook

Mixing pails and paddles

Fig. 4.1 Accessories Before the Act. Before exterior painting starts these accessory materials will be helpful.

ed, dimpled, or coated with non-slip material and should be free of sharp edges.

For fastening wood steps, metal brackets may be used. Steps may also be held in grooves. Two 6-penny nails, or equivalent, should be driven through each end of the steps held in the grooves. Metal steps should be fastened with double rivets. Otherwise, top and bottom steps need metal braces on each side.

The bucket shelf on wood ladders should be able to hold at least 25 lbs. and that of a metal ladder should be able to hold 50 lbs. The shelf should fold within the ladder. Spreaders should be rust resistant.

For a safe stepladder, the distance between rails at the top step should be at least 12 inches, increasing toward the bottom at least one inch per foot of length.

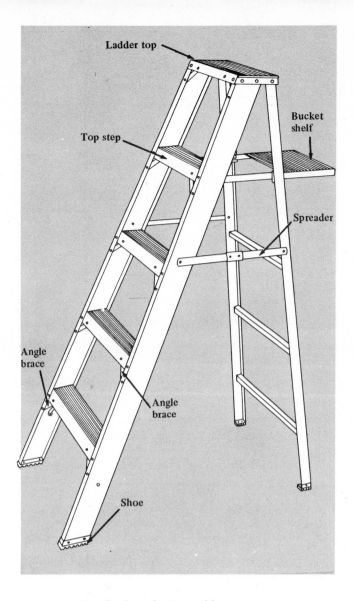

Fig. 4.2 Essentials of a Safe Step-Ladder

Feet should be level in the open position. Metal ladders, in addition, should have feet covered with insulating material.

Test a ladder's stability by climbing to the second or third rung, and while clinging to the side rails, shake it moderately. If it seems loose, try another brand.

Platform Ladder. A short fixed version of the stepladder has a wider top or platform. A scaffold can be made by using these in pairs with a heavy plank between them. They are just high enough to allow a painter or paperhanger to work handily on the ceiling without having to move his ladder every time he advances a few feet. Planks may also be placed between the low rungs of any pair of sturdy, matched stepladders for the same purpose.

Extension Ladders. The heights likely to be climbed are important in selecting an extension ladder. The following table shows a desirable excess length for each range of heights to be reached:

59

Height to be Reached	Length of Sections
9-1/2 ft.–13 ft.	16 ft.
13-1/2 ft.–17 ft.	20 ft.
17-1/2 ft.–21 ft.	24 ft.
21-1/2 ft.–25 ft.	28 ft.
24-1/2 ft.–29 ft.	32 ft.
29 ft.–33 ft.	36 ft.

This chart is based on the need for at least three feet overlap between the highest point you should stand and the highest point of the extension ladder.

Platform
ladder

Fig. 4.3 Platform Ladder

Another overlap factor is the extension of one section beyond the other. If the ladder is up to 36 ft. long, the overlap should be 3 ft.; if it is between 36 and 48 ft., it should be 4 ft.; and between 48 and 60 ft., overlap should be 5 ft.

The Federal Trade Commission now requires ladder manufacturers to clearly mark these figures as to maximum working length and total length of sections.

New metal extension ladders have more safety features than wood and are recommended. Starting with the feet, we note that they have pivoting safety shoes to allow the base to rest squarely, no matter the angle of the ladder. Rungs are rounded but with flat surfaces where the foot rests. (See Fig. 4.4)

In addition to ropes for sliding and securing sections, these ladders have metal rung locks and interlocking side-rail interlocks.

Check upper sections to see that they are at least 12 inches wide. The bottom section should be not less than 12-1/2 inches for ladders up to 16 ft.; 14 inches for those up to 28 ft.; and 15 inches for ladders up to 40 ft.

Correct use of ladders. A few general precautions apply to stepladders and extension ladders.

1. Go up and down carefully, always taking one step at a time.
2. Face the ladder in going up or down.
3. Carry tools or materials in your clothing, or affixed to a belt.
4. Always try to advance your hold on the ladder just before stepping up. Try to hold on to the ladder as feet advance.
5. Place the ladder near the work area. Never over-reach.
6. Near electric circuits, take extra care to keep ladders dry, because they conduct electricity. Severe shocks may result from electric contact.
7. Provide a safe, level footing. Use a brace or lines to safeguard the footing, if necessary.

Safe use of stepladders. The following precautions should be observed while using stepladders:

1. Fully open ladder and make certain the spreaders are locked before climbing.
2. Never go higher than the last step. Standing on the top platform invites loss of balance.

Safe use of extension ladders. The following rules improve the safety of extension ladders:

1. Handle extension ladders to avoid muscle strain. Brace lower end against a solid object. Using both hands, grasp upper end and raise, walking forward as you advance hands under ladder. This raises it to erect position, which makes it easy to move ladder to proper position for painting.
2. Angle of ladder should be such that distance from its base to the wall is one-fourth the distance of a vertical line drawn on the wall from the ground to the top of the ladder. If the vertical distance of this imaginary line is 24 ft., then the ladder should be 6 ft. from the wall. Less distance is too little and may cause the ladder to fall backwards; more will put too much strain on the ladder, possibly causing it to break.
3. Secure the locking device, with eye level with the device to make certain it is fast.
4. Never go so high that it is necessary to reach down to grasp the side rails (always have at least three feet between your feet and the top.)

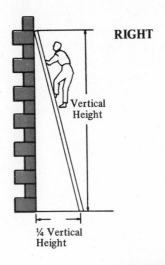

RIGHT

Vertical
Height

¼ Vertical
Height

WRONG

RIGHT

Fig. 4.5 The Right and the Wrong Way to Set Up An Extension Ladder.

Fig. 4.4 Essentials of a Safe Extension Ladder

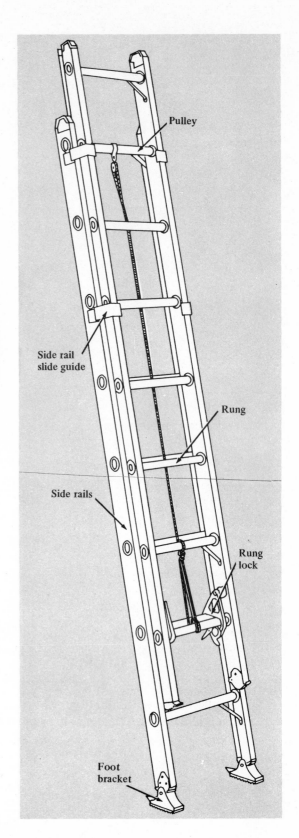

Pulley

Side rail
slide guide

Rung

Side rails

Rung
lock

Foot
bracket

5

It's Easier When
You Paint Right

Most people tend to pooh-pooh painting as an operation that takes only a little brawn and a minimum of brains. That attitude, often resulting in disastrous paint jobs, has boosted the sales volume of a lot of paint manufacturers.

Paint manufacturers are in an unusual business. For competitive reasons, they constantly try to make more durable products to keep customers happy. By so doing, they literally strive to reduce total sales volume. They truly are unhappy when inept paint application causes their products to malfunction, often bringing them unjust blame.

As the careless consumer knocks himself out every two or three years repainting, he blames the paint. But by applying carefully selected paint according to simple procedures, he could postpone his expensive painting job to five or more years. Everybody suffers if he errs, the consumer because he wastes time and money, the paint manufacturer because his good name is undeservedly tarnished.

The Big Decision—BRUSH, ROLLER, FLAT PAD, or SPRAY GUN? Here are some guidelines for selecting a method of application:

Brush. Use a brush:

1. For most primers, particularly where surfaces have tiny irregularities that may be missed by rollers or spray or where penetration is especially important.
2. For corners, edges, and odd shapes.
3. For trim and moulding.
4. For small areas where masking for spray application is not worthwhile.

Rollers. Rollers should be selected:

1. For topcoats where the stippled effect produced by rollers does not matter.

Pour off thin portion into a clean container.

Stir the settled paste, breaking up the lumps, if any. For gallon cans, use a paddle about 1 1/2 inches wide.

Mix thoroughly, using a figure 8 motion. Then follow with a lifting and beating motion.

Continue stirring while gradually returning the poured-off portion to the original container.

Box paint by pouring several times back and forth from one container to the other until uniform.

2. When skilled brush painters are not available.
3. For fairly large areas where masking for spraying would be so extensive that spraying would not pay.
4. For large areas where spraying would create a fire hazard or endanger nearby equipment or personnel.

Flat pad applicators. This method will serve:

1. Any brush job that doesn't require considerable penetration.
2. Any roller job.

Spray guns. These are not always the best and fastest to use. Use them when:

1. Surfaces are large enough so that time lost in masking is more than compensated by the speed in spraying.
2. Surfaces are irregular or round and brush application would be inefficient, or if brush marks must be avoided.
3. When quick-drying lacquer-type coatings are used.
4. For all jobs requiring very smooth finishes.

Rules

A few rules to assure success. Paints, although we rarely take them very seriously, are rather complicated, and often sophisticated chemical compounds and mixtures. They can be temperamental in their reaction to temperature and humidity. Avoid failure by taking the following general rules seriously:

64   1. Paint only when surface and ambient temperatures are between

*Fig. 5.2 This professional painter shows how to paint a wall so that discontinuities
are avoided. Cover areas about two by three feet and then work into the edges as
you expand, before they dry. Work down from ceiling.*

     50° F and 90° F when using a water-thinned coating; and between
     45° and 95° F for other types of coatings.
2. Maintain coatings in container at a temperature range of 65–85° F
    at all times on the job.
3. Paint only when the temperature is expected to stay above freezing
    in the period that the coating is to dry.
4. Paint only when wind velocity is below 15 mph.
5. Paint only when relative humidity is below 80 percent.
6. Observe the recommended spread rate for each kind of coating.
7. Tint each coat differently if the same paint is to be used for successive
    coats in a system to assure complete hiding.
8. Allow sufficient time for each coat to dry before applying another.
9. Allow adequate time for the topcoat to dry before permitting service
    to be resumed.

Coverage. To acquaint users with advantages of the various systems,
rates of coverage of brush, roller, air spray, and airless spray methods
are presented:

Coverage Per Day

Method	Square Feet
Brush	1000
Roller	2000–4000
Air Spray	4000–8000
Airless Spray	8000–12000

Mixing. Paint should be re-mixed before use to correct the inevitable settling of solids in the can. See Fig. 5.1, which shows how the professionals do it. Be certain to avoid foaming. Paint applied with tiny foam bubbles may have popped areas.

Painting Order

In painting a room, get the ceiling coated first, then start in any corner, working down from the ceiling in two to three foot widths. Keep these bands narrow so that the outer edges won't have a chance to dry before you expand to the next section. See Fig. 5.2. If these edges dry, a surface irregularity will result and that looks amateurish. Paint from the dry area into the wet. Trim, doors, windows and moulding should be painted after major surfaces, unless they have narrow under-edges, in which case you paint them first.

Corners and all edges should be painted in strokes that sweep off the edge rather than from the edge inward.

Brush Application

Select a top quality brush if you expect to be proud of your work. High quality natural bristles and synthetic bristles are available for the jobs they suit best. Until recently, natural bristles were indicated for all solvent-thinned paints, and synthetic bristles were limited to water-thinned coatings. Now, a major synthetic fiber manufacturer has perfected bristles suitable for both types of paint.

Of the natural bristles, those from China, consisting of hair from the inner ear of the hog, are considered the best. Until 1972, these were not available to any extent. One of the byproducts of the rapprochement with China is an ample supply of China hog bristles. These, in addition to durability, offer a superior natural "flagging," or forking, which enables the bristle to hold more paint than the lesser natural bristles, mainly those from Poland, and to put down a finer wet-brush mark,

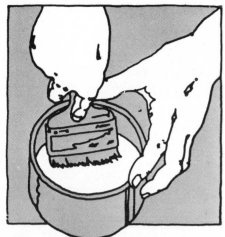

1 After removing excess paint with scraper, soak brush in proper thinner, work it against bottom of container.

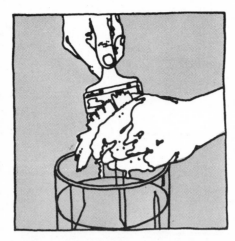

2 To loosen paint in center of brush, squeeze bristles between thumb and forefinger, then rinse again in thinner. If necessary, work brush in mild soap suds, rinse in clear water.

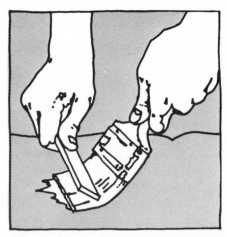

3 Press out water with stick.

4 Twirl brush — in a container so you won't get splashed!

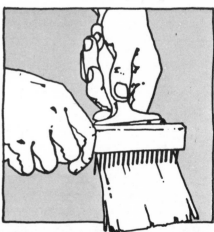

5 Comb bristles carefully — including those below the surface. Allow the brush to dry by suspending from the handle or by laying it flat on a clean surface. Then wrap the dry brush in the original wrapper or in heavy paper to keep the bristles straight. Store suspended by handle or lying flat.

Fig. 5.3 From—U.S. Government General Services Administration.

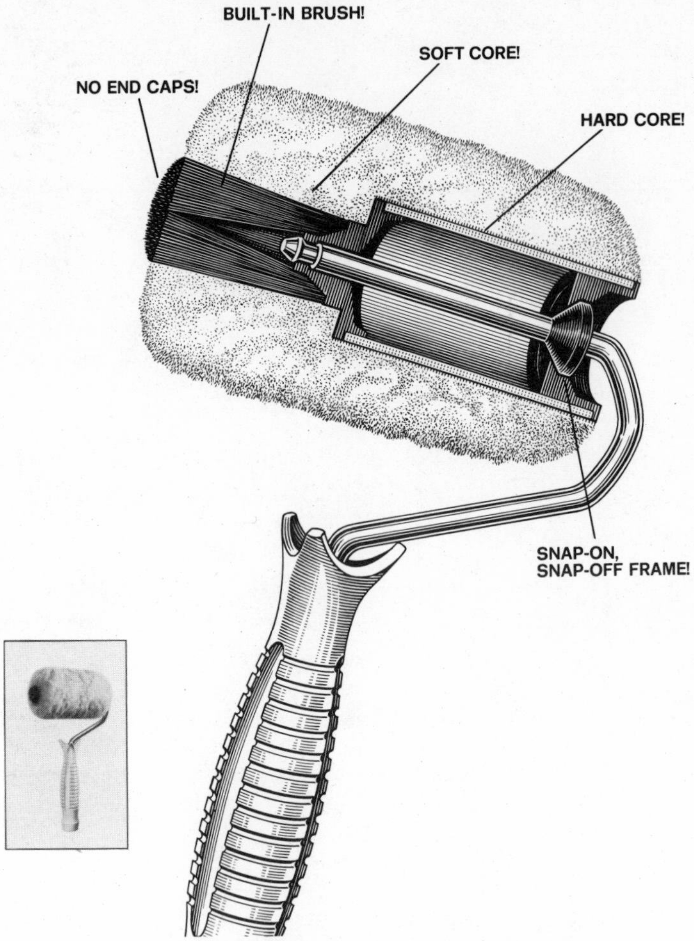

NO END CAPS!

BUILT-IN BRUSH!

SOFT CORE!

HARD CORE!

SNAP-ON,
SNAP-OFF FRAME!

Fig. 5.4 Cutaway of a patented roller. (Speed Painter photo.)

which improves the chances for a smooth film.

Low-priced, bargain brushes found in the promotional bins of many stores are either of horse hair, or blends of low priced hog bristle and horse hair. Horse hair, incidentally, doesn't flag and soon becomes limp and worthless. Avoid it and blends containing it.

Brushes made of badger hair are used for applying varnish, and squirrel and sable-hair brushes are used for fine lines, such as striping and lettering.

Synthetic bristles, mainly of nylon, are split at the end to simulate flagging and are otherwise treated to load paint and leave thin brush marks. Never use them with lacquer, shellac or any paint with a strong solvent. Because they do not swell in water, as do natural bristles, they are preferred for latex paints.

Brush Types. Brushes are designed for specific jobs. The four classes are: 1. wall brushes; 2. sash and trim; 3. enameling and varnish; and 4. stucco and masonry brushes.

Wall Brushes. These are used primarily for large surfaces. They are flat and range in size from 3 to 6 inches.

Sash and Trim Brushes. These are found in round, oval and flat shapes. The flats have a square edge or an angled edge. The rounds

68

MOHAIR HIGH LEVELING ROLLER

Fig. 5.5 Effect of Roller on Leveling. The type of cover material selected for a roller will determine the leveling effect achieved. Note the difference in effects achieved with mohair (left) and a high-leveling roller (right).

are from 1/2 to 2 inches in diameter; the flats range from 1-1/2 to 3 inches wide. For very fine work, chisel-shaped edges are available.

Enameling and Varnish Brushes. Since these must lay down rather viscuous finishes smoothly, they are shorter than other brushes, with finer bristles. They have either flat, square edges, or chisel edges and are two to three inches wide.

Stucco and Masonry Brushes. These resemble flat wall brushes. Nylon is better for rough surfaces. Quality is not important here.

Helpful Notes on Brush Use. Natural bristle brushes should have their bristle portion soaked in linseed oil for 48 hours prior to initial use to swell the fibres in the ferrule so they won't pull out. In loading brushes, dip bristle only halfway in paint to avoid loading the heel. If heel should be loaded, slap brush against something and clear out. Never allow a brush to rest in a paint can. Lay it on a flat surface; and if it is wet with latex paint, wrap in a damp cloth so it won't dry out.

Don't overload a brush in painting, because this may cause sags and runs on the surface. If this occurs, brush out the area, if still tacky, with hard strokes. If dry, sand smooth and repaint. Clean off solvent paints with thinner and remove latex paints with detergent and water. Allow the brush to remain in the cleaner a few minutes, then with fingers work out as much material as possible. Then press out bristles, from top down until bristles are clean.

Before storing a cleaned brush, wash it thoroughly again with soap and water. Use a brush comb to straighten bristles after removing as much liquid as possible by shaking. (See Fig. 5.3)

69

Fig. 5.6 Using Flat Paint Brush to
Paint Under Siding.

Fig. 5.7 Special Flat Brush with
Bristles Arranged to Paint Under
Siding.

Fig. 5.8 Flat Paint Brush in Use.

Fig. 5.9 Flat-Pad Applicator in Use.

Fig. 5.10 Convenient Flat Pad Kit. A handy flat pad combination includes an ingenious feeder-tray with a roller to pick up paint and feed it to pad. A section at end of tray holds putty knife and screw driver.

Roller Application.

Speed is the hallmark of roller application. But make no mistake: you pay for speed in several ways. First, rollers for one reason or another give less coverage per gallon of paint, and most often they yield a light stippled effect that may or may not be objectionable. Finally, for surfaces that require penetration, such as those with chalk, or with irregularities, they are inferior to brushes.

Roller Selection. Rollers differ with respect to width, nap length, and cover material.

Width. Roller fabrics mounted on metal frames are in widths ranging from 1-1/2 to 18 inches. Most common widths are 3 inch, 4 inch, 7 inch, and 9 inches.

Nap Length. Length of fiber, or nap, should be short for relatively smooth results. Medium and rough surfaces require progressively longer naps. Short naps are around 3/16 inch; and long ones are up to 1-1/4 inches.

The following is the suggested nap length for paint types:

Roller Nap Length

Surface	Type of Paint	
	Enamel	Flat
Smooth	3/6"–1/4"	1/4–3/8"
Medium	3/8"	1/2–3/4"
Rough	3/4"	1–1-1/4"

Cover Material. Polyester (Dacron) and modified acrylic (Dynel) fabrics are the most popular materials. Mohair and lamb's wool are also useful for certain purposes.

The following table relates fabric to paint type and surface type:

Table 5.1. Types of Fiber to Use for Various Surfaces.*

Type of Paint	Type of Surface	
	Smooth	Rough
Interior paints		
Latex	Dynel	Dynel
Solvent-thinned	Dynel	Dynel
	Mohair	Lambs' wool
Exterior paints		
Wood	Dacron	Dynel
Other surfaces	Dynel	Dynel
Paints and lacquers		
containing strong solvents	Mohair	Lambs' wool

*From Sidney B. Levinson and Saul Spindel, *Developments in Architectural and Maintenance Painting: A State of the Art Review* (Federation of Societies for Paint Technology: Philadelphia, 1969).

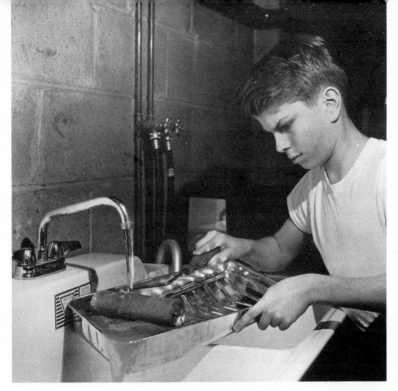

Fig. 5.11 Because acrylic latex paints can be cleaned up with water, instead of solvents, the chore of cleaning brushes and rollers can easily be handled even by a youngster. Recommended procedure is to rinse in plain water, then remove the last traces with a solution of soap or detergent.

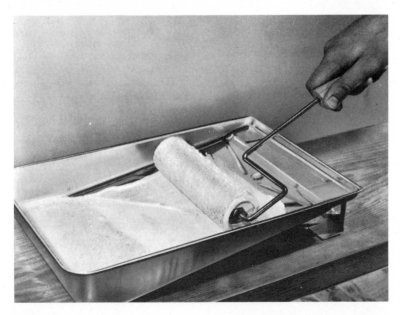

Fig. 5.11a Loading a Roller. Don't roll out the last drop of paint. Return roller to tray and use remaining paint to speed pickup of new load. Keep enough paint in tray so slanted roll-way will provide fast, easy loading. Avoid dripping by loading enough to meet the fiber cover's capacity. A few trial rolls will give you the feel for it.

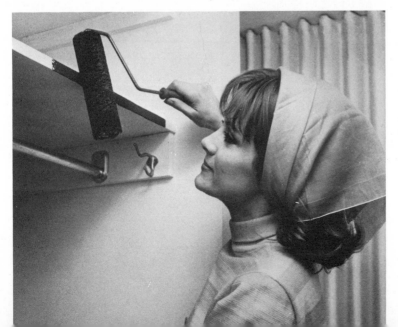

Fig. 5.11b On any flat surface, the fastest way to apply enamels is with a roller. The sag resistance of latex enamels helps assure good appearance. Because they have good leveling qualities, roller marks soon disappear.

73

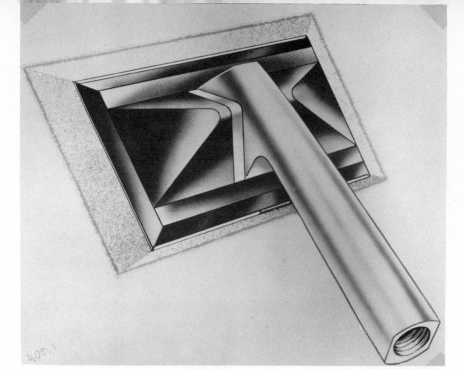

Fig. 5.12 Pad Paint Applicator

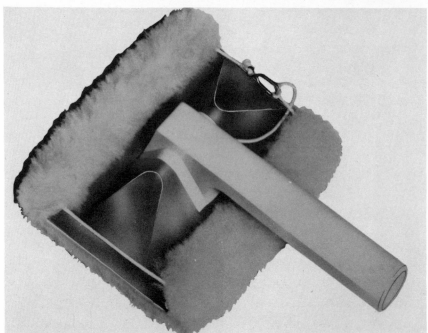

Fig. 5.13 Pad Stain Applicator

In addition to the above fabrics, carpeting on rollers is used for stippling and for applying heavy mastics.

Special Purpose Rollers. Tapered rollers can be bought, with receding edges for ease in painting corners. High-leveling rollers, made of woven fabric, reduce stippling effects and are best for applying latex gloss paints. A new roller has a small brush on its end for coating areas that a roller can't reach, (see Fig. 5.4).

Fence rollers have extra long naps that permit the paint and nap to engulf fence wire so painting can be done from one side. Pipe rollers

Faulty patterns and how to correct them

Pattern	Cause	Correction
	A fan spray pattern that is heavy in the middle, or a pattern that has an unatomized "salt-and-pepper" effect indicates that the atomizing air pressure is not sufficiently high.	Increase pressure from your air supply. Correct air pressures are discussed elsewhere in this instruction section.
	Dried material in sideport "A" restricts passage of air through it. Result: Full pressure of air from clean sideport forces fan pattern in direction of clogged side.	Dissolve material in *thinner*. Do not poke in any of the openings with metal instruments.
	Dried material around the outside of the fluid nozzle tip at position "B" restricts the passage of atomizing air at one point through the center opening of air nozzle and results in pattern shown. This pattern can also be caused by loose air nozzle.	If dried material is causing the trouble, remove air nozzle and wipe off fluid tip, using rag wet with thinner. Tighten air nozzle.
	A split spray or one that is heavy on each end of a fan pattern and weak in the middle is usually caused by (1) too high an atomizing air pressure, or (2) by attempting to get too wide a spray with thin material.	Reducing air pressure will correct cause (1). To correct cause (2), open material control "D" to full position by turning to left. At the same time turn "spray width adjustment "C" to right. This will reduce width of spray but will correct split spray pattern.
Spitting	(1) Dried out packing around material needle valve permits air to get into fluid passageway. This results in spitting. (2) Dirt between fluid nozzle seat and body of a loosely installed fluid nozzle will make a gun spit. (3) A loose or defective swivel nut on siphon cup or material hose can cause spitting.	To correct cause (1) back up knurled nut (E), place two drops of machine oil on packing, replace nut and tighten with fingers only. In aggravated cases, replace packing. To correct cause (2), remove fluid nozzle (F), clean back of nozzle and nozzle seat in gun body using rag wet with thinner, replace nozzle and draw up tightly against body. To correct cause (3) tighten or replace swivel nut (G).

Pointers on cleaning

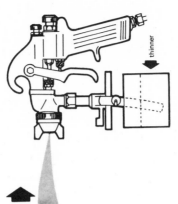

thinner

When the gun is used with a pressure tank or gravity bucket, remove the hose, turn the gun upside down and pour thinner into the fluid opening while moving the trigger constantly. This will flush all passageways.

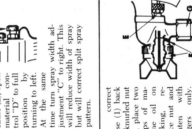

When used with a cup, thinner or suitable solvent should be siphoned through gun by inserting tube in open container of that liquid. Move trigger constantly to thoroughly flush passageway and to clean tip of needle.

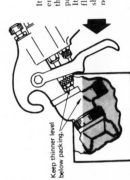

Keep thinner level below packing.

It is extremely poor practice to place an entire gun in thinner. When this is done, the solvent dissolves the oil in the leather packing and causes the gun to spit. It is good practice to place the nozzle and fluid connection in thinner. Vessel used should be shallow enough to prevent thinner from reaching packing.

are actually several small roller covers on one curved wire frame, permitting adaptation to a curved surface.

What to Check Before Buying a Roller. Look for the following:

1. Fabric composition designed for minimum stippling effect. (see Fig. 5.5)
2. Diameter of roller as an index of its ability to pick up a reasonably large quantity of paint per effort.
3. Does nap length suit it for the particular job you have in mind? Don't buy a short nap roller cover if you are to apply a flat paint on a rough surface.
4. Fabric type should be right for the kind of paint and surface you will use. (See Table 5.1)

Conditioning a New Roller Cover. Soak new covers intended for solvent paints by soaking in mineral spirits and squeezing out excess. Another method is to roll the first load of paint out on a piece of paper. Purpose of both steps is to wet fibers and flush out loose lint or dirt.

Cleaning Rollers. Prevent thickening of paint on roller by rinsing occasionally in solvent or water. If using a fast-dry paint, use two rollers, having one soak while the other is in use. (See Fig. 5.6)

Hints on Painting With Rollers. When painting on walls, start with an upward sweep to prevent down-drip. Paint roughly a 2 ft. by 3 ft. area, working up and down, and then even out the paint by rolling horizontally. Don't work until the roller has given up all its paint. Be certain to avoid pushing down so that the last trace of paint is used up. Dip the roller and paint some more.

Rolling on paint outside requires a little horse-sense. If shingles are to be painted, work with the direction in which they run. Flat siding with no grooves or indentations should be covered in horizontal rolls. Those with grooves, etc., should be painted in the direction of the lines. For this kind of work, a long nap roller should be selected. This will assure entry of the paint into the depressions.

Make certain that spaces are all coated. Where there are spaces between rows of shingles, use a brush if the roller can't reach.

Flat Pad Applicators

These consist of a face of some napped fabric, such as mohair, surrounding a base of foam, which serves as the paint reservoir.

These provide probably the fastest application method, other than spray guns. The napped faces have pile depths ranging from 1/2 to 1-3/4 inches and can be used on rough or smooth surfaces.

Pad widths vary from 1″ x 2″ for moulding to 4″ x 7″ for large

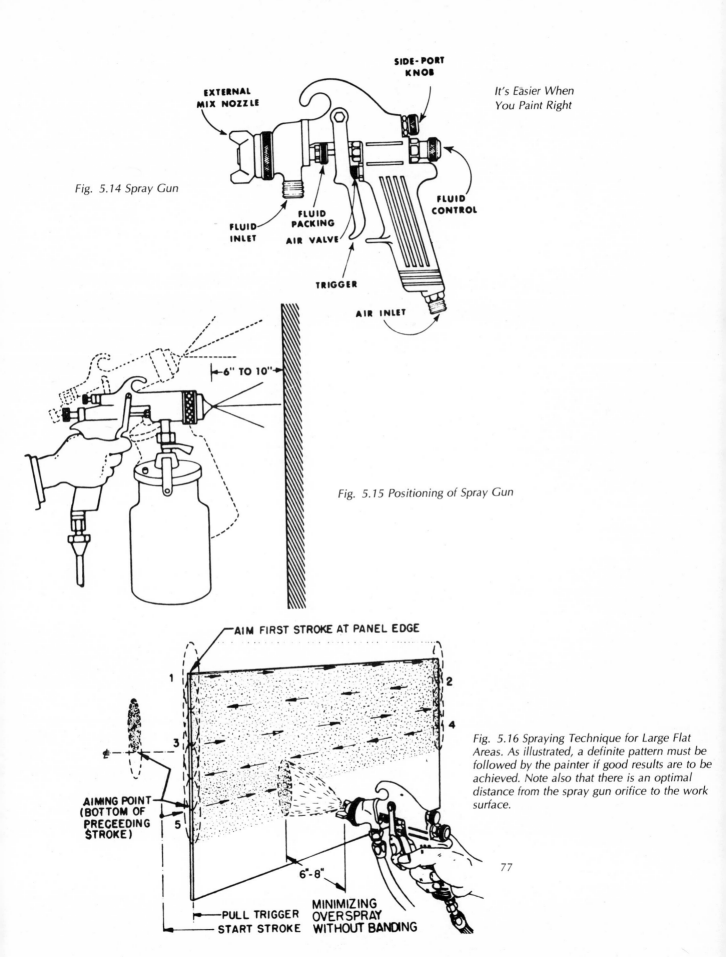

SIDE-PORT KNOB

EXTERNAL MIX NOZZLE

It's Easier When You Paint Right

Fig. 5.14 Spray Gun

FLUID INLET

FLUID PACKING

AIR VALVE

FLUID CONTROL

TRIGGER

AIR INLET

6" TO 10"

Fig. 5.15 Positioning of Spray Gun

AIM FIRST STROKE AT PANEL EDGE

1   2

3   4

5

AIMING POINT (BOTTOM OF PRECEEDING STROKE)

Fig. 5.16 Spraying Technique for Large Flat Areas. As illustrated, a definite pattern must be followed by the painter if good results are to be achieved. Note also that there is an optimal distance from the spray gun orifice to the work surface.

6"-8"

PULL TRIGGER

START STROKE

MINIMIZING OVERSPRAY WITHOUT BANDING

77

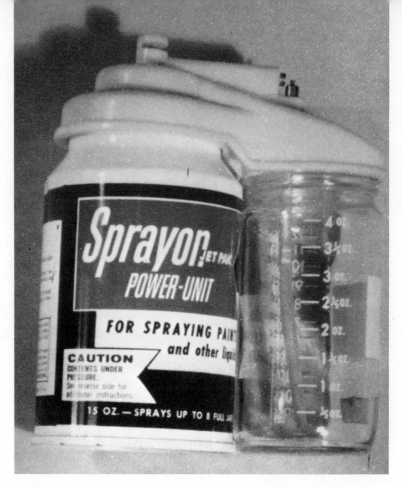

Fig. 5.17 A universal aerosol has its own jar to feed paint through a
charged power-pack.

flat surfaces. Speed is aided by the advantage of paint pickup. The 4"
× 7", for instance, holds about one-third more paint than a 4-inch brush.
(See Fig. 5.9)

For most efficient use, shop for the best tray arrangement. The most
ingenious has a small roller in the tray resembling a printing roller. This
rolls over another roller which is immersed in the paint. The pad picks
up paint by rolling over the larger one.

Flat Pad Types. These are available in stain pads, floor-finish applicators,
mitts and the regular types described above.

Stain pads have a lambs' wool cover over the foam reservoir for
use on shakes, shingles, or panels. Short nap wool is used for smooth
surfaces, and depths up to 1-1/4 inches are available for rough areas.
It has been estimated that these apply stain three times faster than a
brush.

Floor finish applicators have lambs' wool attached to a flat board,
with a 4-foot handle. They are about 3 inches across and 8 to 16 inches
wide. Siding pads are really flat brushes (see Fig. 5.11).

Paint mitts, somewhat like pads, are of lambs' wool and are about
twice as fast as a brush for odd-shapes, such as clover leafs or plumbing-
valve wheels.

78

Care of Pads. Bear in mind that these pads have both a foam reservoir and a napped surface—two materials that can stiffen if paint is left in them after use. So be careful about complete paint removal after each use.

Spray Gun Application.

To get fastest uniform coverage, spray guns are the instruments of choice. However, this speed exacts its price. First of all, equipment is more expensive than brushes, rollers, or flat pads; and guns require more skill and care. Since the deposit of coatings is not precise, adjacent areas must be protected by masking, which is time consuming.

To reduce expense, there are tool rental establishments, which may offer suitable spray guns. And in regard to masking, consideration should be given to the scope of the job. For a few dozen square feet of wall or siding, masking would be an unnecessary bother. For a large area, the time required by masking will, no doubt, be worthwhile. The individual job determines the desirability of spray gun use.

Kinds of Spray Guns. Small guns are relatively inexpensive and can be used for small jobs such as finishing furniture or doors. These are also handy for spraying insecticides. Larger guns offer a variety of nozzles and should be the only type considered for jobs requiring more than a quart or so of paint.

Small, Vibrator-type Spray Guns. These low-volume devices draw paint from a small container—usually attached to the nozzle—by air forced by an electric motor. They are similar to the spray systems possible by attaching a hose, a container and a nozzle to the exhaust end of a flat, canister vacuum cleaner.

These small systems work more slowly than large guns and are inefficient because of their small capacity, but the same rules for applying paint apply to small and large guns alike.

Pressure-feed Spray Guns. The most versatile and safest type of spray gun for most non-professional jobs is the air spray. For professional jobs with very large surfaces, where high-film build is important and where economy of paint use is significant, the so-called airless spray system has advantages.

Non-professionals will be more or less restricted by what they can obtain and learn to use. Principles of use, however, are the same.

Selecting Nozzles. If you plan to use quick-drying paints, you won't want to use the nozzle recommended for thick slower-dry paints. Quick-driers, like water-based paints and lacquers, require a type of nozzle known as the *external mix,* because air and paint are brought together just as they leave the nozzle.

Internal mix nozzles bring the two together inside the nozzle, in   79 effect de-bodying the heavy material and giving it a better chance to deposit uniformly.

Suitable Paint Dilution. Fairly thick paints that are suitable for brush application as they come from the can usually need thinning for spray service. Be certain to read label directions for spray use. No general instructions can be given because each paint manufacturer has his own recommendations.

Adjusting Controls. Get acquainted with your gun before attempting to use it on the surface to be painted. Spray on waste surface to learn how to adjust the nozzle controls to get a uniform deposit of coating.

A *fluid control valve* permits lowering or boosting the flow of liquid, a *spreader control* allows you to set the pattern from round to varying degrees of fan-width. An *air valve* allows you to control the amount of atomization.

Experiment to obtain a satisfactory uniformity of deposit. Too much air results in a thin, runny deposit, particularly in the center of the spray pattern; too little yields a somewhat heavy, dappled effect. Experiment until you have a consistent film that holds to the surface and adequately hides.

Spray-gun Technique. Using a spray gun properly is easy to learn. Always hold it perpendicular to the surface. Aim it at the bottom point of the coating deposited on the previous stroke. Gauge your speed across the surface to the speed of the spray-emission, working back and forth uniformly. Don't pause but keep going, if possible, until the surface is coated.

The extent of your trigger-squeeze will determine spray volume. Hold it at a rate that will enable you to get your desired film at reasonable speed.

Banding Techniques. To reduce paint loss due to overspray, experienced spray operatives use a simple method for handling edges of flat surfaces. At the edges, narrow bands of paint are sprayed so that sweeping horizontal strokes may stop short of the edge, thereby avoiding loss of paint by overspray beyond the edge.

A version of banding takes care of inside corners. Some spray operators work head-on, trying to cover both sides with one motion. Skilled technicians can get an even film that way, but less skilled persons may find it better to band each of the sides, treating each wall as if it had its own edge. Some common sense must be used here too, because overspray from the horizontal strokes as they approach the band would cause excessive build at the corner; so it's smart to make a few quick horizontal strokes adjacent to the band. In that way, these horizontals form a base for building a film at and near the edge. This happens when the regular horizontal strokes deposit their overspray on the horizontals laid down adjacent to the band. Little if any actual spraying will be needed in this area since the overspray will cover these horizontals.

In banding, care should be taken not to make too big a vertical, since these bands should be wet when the horizontal strokes reach them.

Spraying Miscellaneous Surfaces. Not all surfaces are flat. You will run into slender vertical and horizontal surfaces, cylindrical surfaces, and open-faced surfaces. Each of these requires common sense.

Slender Surfaces. Use a narrow horizontal spray pattern by adjusting your gun, or if it seems more desirable, use a narrow vertical pattern.

Cylindrical Surfaces. Here a round pattern is usually best, stroked vertically in lapping strokes, taking care as always that edges are still wet when advancing.

Open Surfaces. Wire and filigree should be backed by a card.

Care of Spray Guns. Be certain to clean the gun after every day's use. To clean, unscrew the feed hose from the paint container. Put the suction tube into the same paint thinner used for the coating. Spray thinner until it comes clear.

If you've been careless and the gun is choked up, you will know because the motor will make a low insistent hum and will probably heat up. Dismantle the equipment crusted with paint and bathe it in thinner. Wet a brush with thinner and remove accessible paint.

Keep the gun adequately oiled in accordance with manufacturer's instructions.

Are Aerosols Worthwhile? Yes, if the surface to be coated is so small that it doesn't pay to go to the trouble of setting up spray or other equipment. An aerosol is far and away the most expensive of all ways of painting. In fact, you get so little paint in an aerosol it verges on the ridiculous. Nevertheless, it is a convenience for small surfaces.

Using Aerosols. Always restudy instructions, although you may have used aerosols frequently. Several hazards must be avoided, especially heat, which may cause the can to explode. The critical temperature is 120 F, which is only 21.4 degrees above body temperature. Protect the can from sharp objects. It is under pressure and if pierced can release great pressure suddenly and dangerously. Finally, beware of inhaling the hydrocarbon solvents and gas. They can damage lung tissue if inhaled to any extent.

Before using, shake the can to allow the small marbles inside to agitate pigment, vehicle and solvent, and shake during use to keep them agitated.

Like professional or vibrator spray equipment, aerosols should be flushed to avoid gumming. Turn the can upside down and let pressure escape by pressing the button, thus clearing the spray head. Failure to do this leaves you with a useless spray can.

6

The Right Paint
for Your Job

The simplest way to buy paint is to visit a neighborhood paint supply store and rely entirely on the operator to select what you need.

That has the advantage of simplicity, but it may not be the best way. The man waiting on you may not be experienced, although oldtimers are pretty well-informed. You may be buying from a large store where the clerks waiting on you cover several products and lack paint knowledge.

You can get better results if you understand a few basic principles of paint selection.

Here's why: The normal paint store operator usually stocks at least two brands and often as many as four or five. He himself may not know which brand offers the best product for your particular requirement. He may even stock four or five brands because the professional painting contractors buying from him have their own favorites, which he must carry.

He may, as a result, be unconcerned about the relative quality of the various brands he handles, knowing that he has built-in sales because of contractor preferences.

It's up to the consumer to know how to judge the products, and up to him to decide whether it pays to purchase a more expensive product because of improved performance.

General Principle. The first general principle in buying paint is that it usually pays to invest in the best available paint for the job. This does not necessarily mean the more expensive. With some knowledge, it should be possible to buy superior paints, sometimes without extra cost. Sometimes a premium price is justified by anticipated results.

Standards for Judging. Three basic rules can be set forth for selecting paint at a retail store. Each requires careful reading of the label that lists ingredients. These labels by law must be accurate. However, most label information about paint constituents must be read carefully.

First the rules, then an explanation of how to use them.

Rule 1—Select the paint of the *type* that you need, which has the *most binder resin.*

Rule 2—Select the paint of the type that you need, which has the *most hiding pigment.*

Rule 3—If one of the paints of the type you need has more binder resin and another has more hiding pigment, decide whether you want the paint to hide more square feet per gallon (because it has more hiding pigment) or whether you want it to last longer (because it has more resin).

Understanding a Few Key Terms. A number of terms are found frequently wherever paint is discussed. The following explanations should be helpful:

1. Primer-sealers, which are used for unpainted surfaces, or those to be repainted after most of the original paint has been removed. These differ from ordinary primers because they have a relatively high percentage of total pigment, which keeps the paint from penetrating.

2. Primers are not intended to seal off porous surfaces but usually have other functions, such as aiding in rust prevention, helping topcoat adhesion, and fixing natural stains in woods such as redwood. They frequently have special pigments such as red lead and must sometimes be checked for safety around young children.

3. Topcoats provide protection against human and natural destruction. By careful selection, topcoats can be found to protect against even the most difficult conditions, such as wind-driven rain, alcohol, acids, alkalis, salt water and salt air, mildew, and intense sunlight.

   For homes, topcoats also play a decorative role. They should not be chosen alone but as part of a whole paint system. Manufacturers recommend specific primers or primer-sealers in a system. It is important that you follow recommendations, because paint failure can result from the wrong combination of primer and topcoat.

4. Flat paint is a kind of topcoat used mainly on large areas where shininess is not desirable. Its flatness, or lack of shine, results from having relatively large quantities of *total pigment.*

5. Gloss paints, or enamels, provide bright surfaces where this is desirable, such as on moulding and trim. Glossy paints are also used extensively for bathrooms and kitchens or wherever moisture is likely to encourage mildew growth.

   Because glossy paints contain higher percentages of binder resin than flat paints, they are also selected for durability. Some very high quality flat paints are actually semi-gloss paint formulations.

Enamel, or gloss, paints are of three types—high gloss, semi-gloss, and eggshell, or satin, which has higher resin content than flat paints but is only slightly shinier.

6. Exterior paints are designed to withstand the ravages of weather and contain materials resistant to the sun. They should withstand sudden temperature changes and the attack of fungus. Flat and enamel paints are available for exteriors.

7. Interior paints are designed to take a fair amount of abuse and scrubbing.

Understanding Paint Materials. As far as the general paint user is concerned, a coating consists of a binder, such as linseed oil or a latex resin; a thinner, such as turpentine, mineral spirits, or water; and a hiding pigment. A few additives and extenders are also used to make paints perform better, either by lasting longer or by helping painters apply them faster, or to help cut cost.

Intelligent decisions about paint selection need a general knowledge of the binder resins used in coatings and the kinds of pigments going into them. Because thinners are selected for their ability to give fluidity to the solids suspended in them, the consumer is concerned with them only insofar as they affect drying time, ease of application, runniness, and paint quality. Extender pigments should not be present to excess. Binder resins and hiding pigments, since they are far more important, will receive primary attention.

Binder Resins. The heart and soul of a paint is the binder. A poor binder or too little good binder inevitably leads to poor performance.

Binders are divided into two general types: those that are thinned with solvents; and those that are reduced with water. The latter are the inaptly named water-based paints, which should really be called *latex emulsion* paints because they are based on emulsions, or suspensions of plastic-like, resinous materials in water. Solvent-thinned coatings are not suspensions at all but actually have oil or oil-like materials dissolved in solvents.

A natural question is: "Which is best, dollar for dollar?" For ultra high performance, premium solvent-thinned binders such as epoxies and urethanes are in a class by themselves, but they are costly and almost never needed for ordinary painting. Solvent-thinned high gloss enamel paints, at this time, are regarded as best in their category, although some latex semigloss enamels are highly regarded. For interior flat paints, latex has virtually taken over. Latex paints perform well outdoors, particularly over cement surfaces (but solvent-thinned rubber paints are better). Latex has made great inroads in all outdoor paints, once almost exclusively dominated by linseed oil and alkyd.

Still, the latter are sometimes preferred if conditions are bad, such as repainting when chalky deteriorated paint is to be coated. New versions of alkyd exterior paints have been introduced recently and are regaining considerable ground from latex paints, despite premium prices.

So, it's impossible to generalize and say that one kind of binder resin is better than the others for all circumstances. Only you know the circumstances that will apply when you paint. In the next two parts of this chapter, we will provide some general guidance in deciding the kind of resins for your job. Later, more detailed specifications should prove helpful in selection.

Solvent-thinned Binders. Some of these dry by combining with oxygen in the air, aided by certain metallic salts, known as catalysts, or driers. The most widely used binder in this class is the alkyd resin family. Members of this family are made by upgrading various vegetable oils, such as linseed oil, soybean, safflower, tall oil (a byproduct of kraft paper manufacture), and castor oil.

Other solvent-thinned binders harden by a chemical reaction taking place when some of their components are brought together just before application. These are called two-component coatings and are usually high performance products.

Important one-package solvent-thinned coatings, in addition to alkyds, are linseed oil exterior paints, rubber-based paints, mainly used for cement surfaces, and phenolics, which are primarily used for metal finishes.

To help you decide which solvent-thinned resin family suits your particular situation, see Table 6.1.

Water-thinned Binders. Even professional painters have almost abandoned solvent-thinned paints for routine interior flat finishes. When highest quality is demanded they may go back to certain premium alkyd flats that take more scrubbing and mauling.

Exterior latex paints and interior and exterior enamels are newer developments that are challenging entrenched solvent-thinned materials. Exterior latex has caught on. Latex enamels have had mixed success. The semigloss paints are growing in importance and have closed the quality gap so that the advantages of easy washup and lack of odor often justifies their use. High gloss latex, though, has a long way to go.

Polyvinyl acetate (PVA) is the major latex in use today. PVA covers a broad range of products, and therein lies an important caution.

PVA always consists of a vinyl acetate component. That one component has to be combined with some other component to make it an effective paint. Several of these work well with vinyl acetate. Others are more than satisfactory for interior latex paints, but are usually not well regarded for exterior coatings.

Acrylic latex emulsion is widely regarded as the best of the currently   85

Table 6.1 Performance Characteristics of Solvent-Thinned Binders.

Use For	Alkyd	Vinyl	2-Pkg. Epoxy	Oil	Phenolic	Rubber Base	Moisture-Cure Urethane
Adhesion	VG	F	E	VG	G	G	G
Hardness	G	G	VG	F	VG	VG	E
Flexibility	G	E	E	G	G	G	VG
Resistance to:							
Abrasion	G	VG	VG	F	VG	G	E
Acid	F	E	G	P	VG	VG	E
Alkali	F	E	E	P	G	VG	VG
Detergent	F	E	E	F	VG	VG	VG
Heat	G	P	G	F	G	VG	G
Strong							
solvents	F	F	E	P	VG	F	E
Water	G	E	G	G	E	VG	VG
Wood	G	NR	G	G	G	NR	G
Fresh, dry concrete	NR	VG	VG	NR	NR	VG	G
Metal	VG	VG	VG	VG	VG	G	G
Interior	G	G	G	G	G	G	G
Exterior							
Rural	G	VG	G	G	G	G	G
Seashore	G	E	VG	G	VG	VG	VG
Industrial areas	F	E	E	VG	VG	VG	VG
Fade resistance	VG	E	G	G	G	G	F
Chalk resistance	G	E	F	G	G	G	F

Source: David Litter Laboratories.
  Key:
  E   Excellent, outstanding
  VG   Very good
  G   Good or average
  F   Fair
  P   Poor
  NR   Not recommended

commercial latex binders, but is also more costly. Consequently, some paints that are described as acrylic paints are really a different formula, polyvinyl acetate/acrylate.

True acrylics contain methyl methacrylate, the component of Plexiglas ® and Lucite ®. This would make them almost rock hard, but to soften this material so it will flow and retain flexibility on drying, a softening ingredient is added.

Semigloss acrylic enamels are unchallenged in the latex field. Acrylics are regarded as the best latex for exterior cement surfaces. Using them for routine interior conditions is rarely necessary because of extra cost.
Cautions for Latex Users. Formulators of latex paints know how to make a thick, buttery latex paint that spreads beautifully and looks rich. Thickening can be accomplished with cellulosic or clay viscosity controllers. They add nothing to paint performance, but may, in excess,

Table 6.2 Salient Facts about Water-Thinned Paints (Latex).

Brushability	E	Gloss retention	°
Odor	Mild	Color, initial	E
Method of cure	Coalescence	Yellowing (clear)	X
Speed of dry		Fade resistance	E
50° F-90° F	E	Hardness	G
Below 50° F	P	Adhesion	G
Film build	G	Flexibility	E
Safety	E	Resistance to:	
Use on wood	E	Abrasion	G
Use on fresh concrete	E	Water	F
Use on metal	NR°	Detergents	G
Min. surface	°	Acid	G
prep'n on metal		Alkali	G
Use as clear	NR	Strong solvents	G
Use in aluminum paint	NR	Heat	G
Choice of gloss	Flat°°	Moisture permeability	High
Service			
Interior	E		
Normal exposure	E		
Marine exposure	F		
Corrosive exposure	NR		

°Exceptions can be used.

°°Acceptable semigloss are available.

Key:

Excellent	E
Good	G
Fair	F
Poor	P
Very poor	VP
Not recommended	NR
Not applicable	X

contribute to failure, since these materials add porosity and water sensitivity.

These thickeners, together with certain improved hiding characteristics of latex paints, may lead the do-it-yourself painter to try to stretch his paint too far. By getting apparently adequate hiding at a spread rate of 500–550 sq. ft. per gallon, the painter may be putting on such a thin coating that little protection is given. Repainting may be required too soon.

This is also important to check when a professional painter is at work. He can cut substantially with water and get maximum spread of a thin coat. You won't know the difference until you need a new paint job a year or so after he leaves. Remember, he's the expensive factor in the job; the paint rarely constitutes more than 10–20 per cent of the cost.

Economics of Coatings Selection. Table 6.3 shows how foolish it is to buy cheap paints. This chart, taken from "Paints and Coatings Handbook" (by Abel Banov, Structures Publishing Co., Farmington, Mich., 1973), written for architects, engineers and contractors, demonstrates that the

Table 6.3 Cost Comparisons for Coatings for Wood Flooring.

	Material Cost/ Sq.Ft.	Labor Cost/ Sq.Ft.*	Life Expect-ancy	Recoat Material Cost/ Sq.Ft.	Recoat Labor Cost/ Sq.Ft.†	Total Cost Per 5 Yrs./ Sq.Ft.
Alkyd	$.008	$.345	1/2 yr.	$.004	$.21	$2.493
Latex	$.016	$.345	1 yr.	$.008	$.21	$1.451
Moisture-Cure Urethane	$.020	$.345	2 yr.	$.010	$.21	$.915
Phenolic Spar	$.010	$.345	1 yr.	$.005	$.21	$1.430
Urethane oil	$.012	$.345	2 yr.	$.006	$.21	.897
Two Component Urethane	$.020	$.345	3 yr.	$.010	$.21	$.732

System consists of two clear coats for total build of 2-mil dry film thickness. Recoat consists of light sand and one coat at 1 mil dry film thickness. Substrate is wood or plastic flooring.

Total costs for five year period with all repairs being light and an additional full coat of original quality at one mil dry film thickness:

Six-month Periods	Alkyd	Latex	Moisture Cure Urethane	Phenolic	Urethane Oil	Two-Component Urethane
0	$.353	$.361	$.365	$.355	$.357	$.365
1	.214					
2	.214	.218		.215		
3	.214					
4	.214	.218	.220	.215	.216	
5	.214					
6	.214	.218		.215		.220
7	.214					
8	.214	.218	.220	.215	.216	
9	.214					
10	.214	.218	.110 (1/2 × .220)	.215	.108 (1/2 × .216)	.147 (2/3 × .220)
Total ($/sq.ft.)	$2.493	$1.451	$.915	$1.430	$.897	$.732

*Labor cost per sq.ft. = $.065—miscellaneous labor; $.15—sanding; $.13—two-coat application by roller or brush = $.345.

†Recoat labor cost per sq.ft. = $.15—light sand; $.06—one coat by hand or spray = $.21.

Sources: Derived from C. H. Kline Report, Stanford Research Institute *Chemical Economics Handbook*, market surveys. Chart developed by Mobay Chemical Co.

labor cost per square foot is so great that repainting should have to be done as infrequently as possible.

Notice that the labor to apply the low-cost alkyd paint was the same as for the three premium paints. The lowest total cost per square foot for 10 years was achieved by the uralkyd paint (an upgraded alkyd binder that combines the better features of this workhorse with those of urethanes at a modest increase in price). Because it has a better spread rate, it cost only one-half cent more per sq. ft. than the less expensive alkyd. But the uralkyd has a life expectancy of five years, compared with two for the low-priced alkyd used in the study. The chlorinated rubber-modified alkyd had a substantially lower cost per square foot than the alkyd but not as favorable as the lower-cost latex and the uralkyd. These better results were obtained because the alkyd required brush-cleaning and repainting every two years; and the others needed it less often. The paint cost was almost insignificant when stacked against the labor cost for the initial paint job and the recoat work.

Unfortunately, it is difficult to find uralkyds in retail stores, but an even better exterior paint based on silicone-modified alkyds is now offered fairly widely. Life expectancy, outweighing extra cost, is greater, making the economics favorable. Silicone alkyds with about 10 years life, incidentally, now play a prominent role in military specifications.

In summary, remember that whether you or a contractor do the job, paint is a small cost factor. Muscle power, yours or the contractor's, is worth money. Use less by buying better paint.

How to Read a Paint Label. Getting the most paint value for your money requires just a little attention to what is usually on your paint label—no matter if it's often in small type. Almost all paint from reliable manufacturers lists components on the can. This list is usually on the back of the label, near the bottom.

With perfectly honest intentions, those who provide this information use a traditional format that can be misleading. It's up to you to penetrate the verbiage, and it's easy.

Here's what to look for and why. First, check out the amount of binder resin and hiding pigment. Why? Because a paint of a *given type* with more binder is almost always better than one with less; and a paint with more hiding pigment will almost always cover more square feet than another with less.

But you can't just look at the label, usually, and determine either the binder or the hiding pigment. You have to make simple mathematical computation that can be done by an elementary school youngster.

First, to learn the percentage by weight of binder content, you look for the line that reads *total vehicle,* which means binder resin plus thinner. If one latex flat interior paint, for example, has *total vehicle* of 64.8 per cent, the next line on the label informs you that only 25.1 per cent of that is actual binder resin; and then you know that you can look around and possibly get a better paint from the same manufacturer. Table 6.4 shows two flat latex interior paints from the same major firm. This firm, like most others, offers more than one grade of most paints for   89 competitive reasons, not because they want to offer less than the best.

The lesser latex has only 16.26 per cent of the total paint as binder resin, while the better one has 23.1 per cent, or almost half again as much.

(Find this by multiplying the *total vehicle* figure—64.8 per cent or 0.648 by 25.1 per cent or 0.251).

Table 6.4 also shows that the lesser paint has 35.2 per cent as *Total Pigment Content,* which consists of hiding pigment and filler. You want as much hiding pigment as you can get for a wall paint so it will cover more wall.

The lesser paint has more *Total Pigment,* since we already know that it has less durability-inducing resin. But it has much less hiding pigment (53.4 per cent), while the better paint has 91.4 per cent of its Total Pigment as hiding pigment.

Here it is: 53.4 per cent (or 0.534) times 35.2 per cent (0.352) equals 0.187 or 18.7 per cent. And the better paint has 91.4 per cent (0.914) times 25.6 per cent (0.256) equals 0.233 or 23.3 per cent hiding pigment.

The paint with more resin will, as a result, take more beating, permit more scrubbing, and will be more likely to adjust to stresses and strains in the surface resulting from temperature changes or mild swelling because of moisture. More hiding pigment will mean that your paint will go further.

Paying a dollar or two more for the better paint will probably assure longer life and may cost little if any more per square foot because it will cover more ground.

With this brief lesson in determining the binder resin content and the hiding pigment content of various paints, you can make a value judgment before purchasing one product in preference to another.

We now turn to considerations in purchasing coatings for various surfaces, exterior and interior.

Since in many instances, the same paints can be used for interior or exterior, particularly primers, the discussion on selection of coatings will be divided into types of surface: cement, metal, and wood. Differences in material for exterior and interior will be covered in the appropriate sections.

To simplify selections, charts will be used to compare the components in various kinds of paint for particular surfaces. Wherever possible, these will be compared with specifications contained in "Paints and Coatings Handbook," prepared for architects, builders and maintenance engineers involved professionally in the use of paint. An effort has been made to use standards established in the book as guides for users of this volume. In the tables, GPC numbers are the designation used in "Paints and Coatings Handbook."

(It should be added that a number of excellent paint manufacturers

Table 6.4 Comparison of Composition of Two Flat Latex Paints, Interior

Binder	Total Vehicle As % of Paint	Binder As % of Vehicle	Total Pigment Including Filler	Hiding Pigment As % of total Pigment
Poly-Vinyl Acrylate	64.8%	25.1%	35.2%	53.4%
Poly-Vinyl Acrylate	74.4%	31%	25.6%	91.4%

do not list components on their labels. In these instances, the reputation of the manufacturer and the confidence you have in your paint dealer will have to be sufficient for selecting a paint.)

Selecting Coatings for Exterior Cement Surfaces. This category of exterior coatings covers concrete, concrete block, cinder block, brick, stucco, masonry, and asbestos cement shingles.

All of these materials have two characteristics which are important in selecting protective coatings. First, they are all porous to a greater or less degree, and second, they are alkaline.

Their porosity means that primers should be selected so that excessive penetration and waste will be prevented.

Their alkalinity demands that alkaline-sensitive products be avoided. To put it positively, it means that latex paints, which work well with alkaline materials, have an advantage over alkyds and oil paints, although the others may be used under some circumstances. (See Chapter 3.)

It also means that rubber-based paints (styrene butadiene, styrene acrylate, and chlorinated rubber—all alkali-resistant), which are notably good on alkaline surfaces, provide advantages.

Another characteristic of cement surfaces is their ability to pass water vapor from inside a structure. For that reason, paints that permit a house to breathe are needed. The latex and the rubber paints have that characteristic. Some solvent-thinned paints, those with lead and zinc salts, tend to form hard, impenetrable films through which water-vapor cannot pass.

For priming, very often topcoat finishes can be used by simply thinning them, permitting the liquid to flow in and around the tiny rough spots and voids that would otherwise cause pinholes to form in the finish. Pinholes would allow liquid-phase water (the kind that descends as rain) to enter and possibly attack the surface. If the rain is converted soon to gas phase (water vapor), it will work its way out harmlessly. However, it may stay as water and absorb alkali chemicals in the concrete, or brick, or shingle and then work its way out, causing damage to the paint. (See Chapter 2.)

Table 6.5 Guide to Selection of Exterior Cement Coatings

Binder		Total Vehicle As % of Paint	Binder As % of Vehicle	Total Pigment Including Filler	Hiding Pigment As % of total Pigment	Source*
P-1 (Flat)	Acrylic	62%	29%	38%	60%	GPC 23 TTP 19
P-2 (Flat)	Acrylic	62.1%	40%	37.9%	64%	Commercial
P-3 (Satin)	Acrylic	75.9%	29.7%	24.1%	92.6%	Commercial
P-4 (Flat)	Vinyl Acrylate	68%	20%	32%		GPC 26 TTP 55
P-5 (Flat)	Vinyl Acrylate	65.8%	50%	34.2%	70.6%	Commercial
P-6 Primer- Sealer	Vinyl Acrylate	67.5%	57.5%	32.5%	93%	Commercial
P-7 (Flat)	Oil or Alkyd	40%	40%	60%	60–65%	GPC 24 TTP 24
P-8 (Flat)	Oil or Alkyd	40.5%	78.1%	59.5%	34.8%	Commercial
P-9 (Clear)	Phenolic & Tung	100%	50%			Commercial
P-10 (Condi- tioner)	Tung- phenol.	70%	93%	30%	16.7%	Commercial
P-11 (Filler)	Styrene Butadiene	41.8– 45.8%	17.2%	54.2– 58.2%		GPC 33 TTF 1098
P-12 (Water- Proofing)	Vin.Tolu. Butadiene	35.5– 39.5%	21.5– 25.5%	60.5– 64.5%	6%	GPC 36 TTP 1411
P-13 (Moist- Condit'ns)	Chlor. Rubb. or Styr. Acryl.					GPC 28 TTP 95
P-14 (Gloss)	Urethane					GPC 20 TTC 542
P-15 (Clear)	Urethane					GPC 18 TTC 540
P-16 (Gloss)	Epoxy Polyamide					GPC 13 TTC 535

*GPC numbers from "Paints and Coatings Handbook." Other designations are federal specifications.

Exterior Cement Surfaces, Ordinary Conditions. Numerous excellent exterior coatings are available to meet normal conditions. Most of them are superior to those required by U.S. Government specifications. This is illustrated by Table 6.5. Product P-1, based on a Federal specification, has less binder vehicle and less hiding pigment than a representative commercially available product listed as P-2 in the table.

Similarly, the vinyl acrylate specification is lower in quality than the corresponding commercial specification.

Intense competition and constant advances in coatings technology have added up to a wide selection of excellent products for the consumer who takes the trouble to assure himself that he has the best.

Table 6.5 is not all-inclusive by any means. Certain major and regional companies utilize other binders, some of them unique to the companies. If the company has a top reputation, you may be certain that its good name has been protected by ample research and development before the product was introduced.

Even at that, comparison shopping will help the consumer understand which of the various grades offered is preferable.

An interesting product, listed as P-3, should be studied a moment. Its total vehicle content is listed as 75.9 per cent, with 29.7 percent of that consisting of acrylic binder. The product is described as a satin finish, which means that it is not quite as flat as a flat-paint but not nearly as glossy as a semigloss. This type of paint, as can be seen, has more binder than the regular flat acrylic, P-2, and has more hiding pigment. The price is not much greater, but its wear potential is notably better.

Exterior Cement Surfaces, Special Conditions. When a clear protective coating is required, a phenolic-tung, P-9 in Table 6.5, provides a shield against blows and weather. Other clear proprietary products are available based on silicones or acrylics.

When chalking paints on cement surfaces must be repainted, conditioners serve as tie-coats for the topcoats so that the new coats won't lift off the old paint. Some, such as P-10, are made of tung-phenolic resins; others are based on linseed-alkyd and rubber resins dissolved in solvents. These are specially formulated to penetrate the existing finish and hold it to the surface. Not all stores handle these rubber-based products, and it may be necessary to inquire ahead a few days so that the material can be ordered.

Concrete and cinder blocks, because of their large pores, pose special problems in coating. Unless fillers are used, these pores will drink up paint like a thirsty camel. Use of fillers, represented by P-11, kills thirst.

With proper filling, a concrete or cinder block surface, top-coated with a heavy paint based on the same resin, P-12, successfully withstood the equivalent of 70-gallons of water per hour driven by 100 mph winds. Because P-12 contains cement and has the appearance of a thick filler, some people incorrectly use it in place of a filler. It doesn't work. (See Fig. 6.1)

Swimming pools and moist conditions require special paints formulated to reduce porosity to the barest minimum. Hard, usually glossy, coatings with unusually large percentages of resin are required for this purpose. P-13 on table 6.5 permits the manufacturer to use a wide variety

*Fig. 6.1 High-Build Coating for Irregular Cement Surfaces. High-build coatings
primed with fillers help smooth this rough cinder block.*

of materials plus either styrene acrylate or chlorinated rubber. For Federal
Specification TTP 95, an exacting test is prescribed. It may be desirable
to ask the store operator furnishing this material to check with his source
to determine if his product meets this federal standard.

Salt spray and chemical environments require chemical-resistant
paints. P-16 represents a reasonably priced chemical resistant coating
that also provides impact and abrasion resistance. A more expensive
material based on a polyester epoxy can also be obtained for extreme
conditions. These are two-package coatings, which means that a curing
agent is held in a separate container in storage. The two parts are brought
together just prior to application.

Selecting Coatings for Exterior Metal Surfaces. Consumers seeking paints
capable of rust-prevention have been under a handicap since Jan. 1,
1973, when federal laws virtually eliminating lead from paints to be used
around households went into effect.

Lead oxides for centuries have been the key weapon in the defense
against rust. Now, satisfactory paints have been formulated for rust-
prevention and the chances are good that they will measure up. We
have compiled a list of lead-free primers and topcoats from established
federal specifications which can serve as a guide for proven paints that
are currently offered. Finding these at neighborhood paint stores should
not be difficult, but they probably can be ordered if they are not in
stock. Most stores have replacements for standard lead-containing over-
the-counter metal paints.

Primers are really the main concern because they do most of the
work in systems suitable for the relatively simple problems encountered
around homes. Topcoats serve as important shields for the primers that
contain the vital pigmentation that protects by virtually sacrificing itself.

The key to metal protection is the maintenance of an intact surface.
A good metal coating system should be free of pinholes and it should
be non-porous so that water can't percolate down to the metal.

94 Yet, blows do crack paint and scratches do penetrate below the

Table 6.6 Guide to Selection of Exterior Metal Coatings

	Binder	Total Vehicle As % of Paint	Binder As % of Vehicle	Total Pigment Including Filler	Active Pigment As % of total Pigment	Source
P-17 (Zinc Yell. Primer)	Linseed & Alkyd	44%	94%	56%	70%	Commercial
P-18 (Zinc-Rich)	Epoxy Ester	21%	67%	79%	79%	Commercial
P-19 (Zinc Ox. Prim-Topc.)	Lins'd Oil	39–41%	76%	59–61%	34% +23% Hiding	GPC 41 TTP 105
P-20 (Prim-Topcoat)	Chlor. Rubber	9–50%	90%	50–91%	98.5%	GPC 58 TTP 1046
P-21 (Prim.-Topcoat)	Acrylic					Commercial
P-22 (SemiGl.)	Silicone Alkyd	Binder should be 58% of total weight				GPC 45 TTE 490
P-23 (Enamel)	Urea or Melamine Alkyd		49–50%	No extenders		GPC 44 TTE 489

surface. That's when water, the culprit in rust formation, can go to work.

Rust-inhibiting or rust-preventing pigments work by taking over the brunt of the attack. Thus, they are sometimes said to be *sacrificial,* or *passivating.* They, in effect, work on a sort of a ranking of metal society, with "pecking orders." Certain metals, starting with gold and platinum, are high in the order of noble metals. Iron and iron oxide (which is the chemical term for rust) are somewhat higher on the scale than zinc. Therefore, you will notice in P-18 and P-19 of Table 6.6 that zinc is the major factor. When water and oxygen from the atmosphere work their way down to the iron or steel surface, zinc in the coating sets up a passive defense and reacts with these spoilers.

The chances are pretty good that you will not need such high quality and expensive primers as these. P-17 or others provided by established paint manufacturers should be adequate; but for truly serious situations paints of the more effective type may be needed, and it may be necessary to have them ordered.

Those readers concerned with industrial structures or boats are not affected by lead-limits. Numerous excellent primers and topcoats containing red lead oxide or basic silico-lead-chromate, or molybdates, are readily available for use where children are not likely to come in contact with the paint. This applies to boat paints and other materials required for metal subjected to moist environments.

You will notice that all of these paints have high percentages of binder and pigment. These are heavy materials, using heavy pigments. It is advisable to select a system with a required primer and a recommended topcoat. Topcoats should be matched to the primer. Since many metal topcoats are enamels (because maximum protection is desirable, the high percentage of binder in enamels makes them tougher and more resistant to attack), it is important that manufacturers' recommendations for matching primer and topcoat be observed.

This brings up the matter of *enamel holdout,* which can ruin the appearance of an enamel. Primers can cause this condition if they are not properly matched to the topcoat. If the primer is too susceptible to thinner or binders in the enamel, it will absorb some of them. This will upset the ratio of binder to pigment in the topcoat and cause inconsistent gloss.

In addition, it has been found that if the wrong topcoat is used with a primer, any moisture entering the system will have trouble leaving the primer through the topcoat. Trapped moisture has been found responsible for accelerated rusting.

What this means is that paint systems are needed, including primers and recommended topcoats.

Excellent systems based on alkyds, epoxies, urethanes, and chlorinated rubber are on the market, free of lead.

With the exception of the alkyds, they require extreme care in surface preparation, and very likely will need a professional applicator. It is entirely probable, however, that hand or mechanical wirebrushing can be done by the do-it-yourselfer, if he applies his coating immediately after preparation and does not allow moisture in the atmosphere to start working on the surface.

Where it is probable that moisture will reach the surface before paint is to be applied, it may be desirable to use an acrylic paint listed as P-21. Because it is water-thinned, it will incorporate any moisture on the surface.

Two lead-free topcoats that have been proven in federal specifications are P-22, a semigloss silicone alkyd, and P-23, a urea or melamine-modified alkyd, similar to materials that are widely offered. Most major companies offer these, so they can be ordered if not on hand.

While emphasis has been placed on enamel topcoats, flats are also available.

You will notice that, unlike the section on cement surfaces, metal coatings for ordinary and problem areas have been treated together. That's because *all* metal surfaces are problems.

Fig. 6.2 Painting Galvanized Materials. After unprimed galvanizing has weathered enough to remove stain-inhibitor applied at factory, prime with a zinc oxide-zinc dust primer and then topcoat.

However, some are more problem-causing than others.

Galvanized metal, for example, requires a primer similar to P-19, except that zinc dust is combined with zinc oxide. P-20 with chlorinated rubber and zinc dust is also suitable. It is important that galvanized metal weather for about six months without paint to work off an inhibitor often applied at the factory to keep moisture from staining the unprimed galvanizing.

If this inhibitor is not removed before painting, paint will flake off after a while, particularly if the surface is subject to wide temperature fluctuations.

For aluminum, tin, copper, or brass, a linseed oil or phenolic-based primer will be needed. First, however, these metals should be treated with a conditioner made up of polyvinyl butyral and phosphoric acid.

Primers for opaque finishes on these metals have lead-containing pigments. Usually, however, these metals are coated clear; and several resins have been formulated into suitable one-coat clears, notably silicone, acrylic, epoxy, and urethane. But don't forget the pretreatment described above.

(For rugged atmospheric conditions, such as those encountered in industrial areas, sophisticated coatings requiring complicated techniques are needed. These are beyond the province of this book. Persons requiring this information are referred to *Paints and Coatings Handbook.*)

Selecting Coatings for Exterior Wood Surfaces. Because wood is a complex material, consisting of alternate bands of spring and summer growth, which vary in their rate of expansion and contraction, coatings used on them must be capable of reacting to varying rates of stress.

97

Table 6.7 Guide to Selection of Exterior Wood Coatings

	Binder	Total Vehicle As % of Paint	Binder As % of Vehicle	Total Pigment Including Filler	Active Pigment As % of total Pigment	Source
P-24 (Prim. Topc't)	Linseed Oil	39–41%	76%	59–61%	34% +23% Hiding	GPC 41 TTP 105
P-25 (Wood Stain Inhib.)	Acrylic	Must have special acrylic additive E-726 and zinc oxide				GPC 66
P-26 (Wood Sealer)	Varnish or Oil	At least 40% binder				GPC 68 TTS 176
P-27 (Shake, Shingle, Siding)	Alkyd	47–53%	32%	47–53%	21% +42% Hiding	GPC 67 TTP 52
P-28 (Trim, Doors & Shutters)	Alkyd	63–92% (Depends on color)	43–60%	8–37%		GPC 64 TTP 37
P-30 (Stain)		From any reputable manufacturer.				

That's just one little problem. The other is the need to prevent certain dye-containing woods, like redwood and cedar, from working into primers and topcoats and discoloring the surface. Before Jan. 1, 1973, when federal limits on lead pigments became effective, a white pigment, lead carbonate, effectively took care of this problem. Now, a few substitutes have appeared. They seem to be working.

Most modern topcoats are sufficiently flexible to meet the varying stresses to which they will be subjected. Flat and gloss paints are available in great abundance. The gloss paints are generally known as trim paint, sometimes as trim and trellis paint. They are mainly used around doors and windows, soffits, and for doors. P-28 in Table 6.7 is a typical trim paint.

Shake and shingle paint has to be particularly good quality because problems often arise from moisture working behind the siding and then fighting its way through the wood and the paint. P-27 is a representative shake and shingle coating.

Notice in the coatings in Table 6.7 the final column heading reads "active pigment as a percent of total pigment content." That's because pigments in wood coatings play an active role in the formulation. While they may also hide, as in the case of the zinc oxide used in P-24 and P-27, their main role is to react with the alkyd resin and form zinc soaps that fix the chemicals in wood.

In P-25, a wood stain inhibitor contains a special chemical developed by Rohm & Haas, the major source of acrylic technology, to block wood stains, including knot saps. Here, too, zinc oxide is used.

Seal coats are important where the natural look of wood is desired. P-26, containing at least 40 per cent of varnish or linseed oil, effectively prevents water from entering the wood surface.

This is also an important requirement for new, unpainted plywood. Then, with this as a primer, at least two coats of a high quality acrylic should be used (P-2 or P-3 of Table 6.5).

Plywood is susceptible to moisture, and because this can wreck the adhesives used for laminating the plies, it is extremely important that exterior-grades of plywood be sealed at their end-grains. A top quality exterior primer, represented by P-24, should be used for this purpose.

A second coat of P-24 will help assure the integrity of the end grains, and hence, of the plywood.

Sanded plywood should always be painted, while unsanded plywood may be painted or stained.

Textured plywood preferably should be stained because the grooves that are almost certainly present yield a myriad of end-grains, which are areas where the bands of growth in the wood have been cut and exposed. It is here that moisture is most likely to enter. Because stains are mostly binder, they offer maximum protection.

Stains are readily available. They are varnish binders colored with transparent iron oxide or dyes, which allow the natural beauty of the wood to come through.

Selecting Coatings for Interior Surfaces. While certain situations require specialized interior coatings, conditions, in general, are such that a few paints can take care of most requirements for interior walls, doors, and trim.

Fig. 6.3a

Know Your Wood Grain. Open-grain wood (left) requires filling. Note the broken grain, usually indicative of this type. Close grain wood (right) has more continuous texture, needs no filler.

*Fig. 6.3b Fill Holes and Cracks. Holes
cracks should be smoothed over with
patching compound. Plastic wood,
powdered wood in a synthetic resin ba.
comes close to matching texture of woo*

Fig. 6.3c

*Machines Aid Floor Refinishing. Badly worn, discolored or chipped floor surfaces
require complete removal of the finish. Hand sanding is impractical. A large
drum-type sanding machine with vacuum attachment for the main floor area and a
power edger (above) can be rented. Great care is needed to avoid gouges. Two or
three sandings are needed, each with finer grit than the previous one. Sand with the
grain. Even with an edger-sander, hand scraping is sometimes needed at the edges
(right above).*

Compared to exterior conditions, interiors have it easy. No rain, wind,
sand, dust, dirt or fungus with which to contend. Only an occasional
cuff from a youngster, or smears of jam or chocolate ice cream, which
can be removed, although Mother may verge on a nervous breakdown
in the process.

The five basic purposes of interior coatings can be summarized as
follows:

1. To improve appearance.
2. To enhance sanitation efficiency.
3. To aid illumination and visibility.
4. To protect subsurfaces.
5. To boost safety.

Everyone has his own order of priorities. Appearance will come first with many families, while there are those who would say that a bathroom requires less consideration of appearance than a living room. Sanitation and quick, easy cleanup should be the prime consideration in buying a paint for a bathroom. Fortunately, this can be had along with excellent appearance.

Illumination may be the first choice for a sewing room, or where card games are frequently held. Sanitation should be important in a kitchen where efficient cleanup is required, but the woman of the house usually also wants good illumination, so a glossy coating may be needed.

Everyone has his own idea about the most important considerations in selecting an interior paint, and he should also have his own ideas for each room.

Cement, Metal and Wood Coatings.   Many interior coatings can be used for all three classes of surfaces. True, special conditions require special coatings for each. Most of these special situations require high performance coatings—urethanes, epoxies, polyester epoxies, and phenolics. These will be found in Table 6.5, listed from P-9 to P-16. Help in selection of these will be found in the preceding sections covering exterior cement, metal and wood coatings.

Wall Paints, Flat.   These are the common workhorses of the trade. At one time, alkyd flats were king. Now, latex flats have taken over. These are mostly polyvinyl acetate-based materials, but styrene butadiene emulsion paints are sold in great quantity by one of the largest manufacturers. These rubber paints, a water-thinned version of one of the toughest synthetics, have stayed popular despite being abandoned by most producers.

While we said that alkyd flats no longer lead in wall paints, don't write them off. Aside from the excellence of the workhorse grades, some paint manufacturers now offer outstanding flat enamels, which seems a contradiction in terms. Enamels, as has been pointed out, have considerably more binder resin than flat paints; so for the flat enamels, formulations that have enough binder to classify as glosses are flattened with silica flatting agents, which do not affect performance. The wall has all the scrubbability and durability of an enamel without the gloss.

Notice that P-35, a commercially available flat enamel, has 40.2 per cent Total Vehicle, with 75 per cent of that consisting of binder, which usually is soybean oil alkyd, the most costly and desirable.

Compare this with a typical commercial flat wall alkyd, P-34, which has substantially less. Also, you will note, P-35 only has 58.8 per cent Total Pigment as against 68 per cent for P-34; and it has 47 per cent of Total Pigment as hiding pigment versus only 23.2 percent for P-34.

Paint industry people, including the author, tend to select this type   101

Table 6.8 Guide to Selection of Interior Paint—All Surfaces

	Binder	Total Vehicle As % of Paint	Binder As % of Vehicle	Total Pigment Including Filler	Hiding Pigment As % of total Pigment	Source
P-31 (Wall, Flat, Self Prim'g)	Acrylic	59.8%	28.7%	40.2%	48.5%	Commercial
P-32 (Satin Self-Prim'g)	Acrylic	75.9%	29.7%	24.1%	92.6%	Commercial
P-33 (Wall, Flat, Self Prim'g)	Polyv. Acet.	63.8%	35.8%	36.2%	62.5%	Commercial
P-34 (Wall, Flat)	Alkyd	32%	38%	68%	23.3%	Commercial
P-35 (Wall, Flat, Enam.)	Alkyd	40.2%	75%	58.8%	47%	Commercial
P-36 (Semigl.)	Alkyd	68.4%	48.6%	32.6%	59.2%	Commercial
P-37 (High Gloss)	Alkyd	71.8%	60.5%	28.2%	99.4%	Commercial
P-38 (Semigl. Self-Prim'g)	Acrylic					Commercial

For High Performance Coatings See Table 6.5, Products identified as P-9, P-10, P-11; P-12; P-13; P-14; P-15; and P-16, as required.
For Metal and Wood Primers, other than where self-priming is used, see Table 6.6 and Table 6.7.

of wall paint, because the small premium price is more than justified.

While PVA may be the most popular interior latex wall paint, true acrylics, as opposed to polyvinyl acrylates that are sometimes erroneously described as acrylics, are highly regarded where the extra cost is unimportant.

P-31 in Table 6.8 is a typical acrylic flat wall paint. It has a healthy slug of binder solids and restraint in the use of filler pigments. It should be less expensive than P-32, which like P-35 is a satin, or slightly glossier wall paint. Since we've established that the more binder resin the tougher and more durable the paint, P-32, with its larger percentage of binder than P-31, should take more scrubbing and abuse. You will also notice that, in addition to more binder solids, it also has a far greater percentage of hiding pigment in its Total Pigment.

You will also notice that P-31 has a larger percentage of Total Pigment, including filler. That means that it will be more porous than P-32 and will absorb more moisture from the atmosphere, and will be more likely to pass moisture from a kitchen, a bathroom or a laundry room through the wall and on to the air space between walls and then, in the form of water vapor, through the exterior walls of a house.

In a bathroom, kitchen, or laundry room, it is also more likely to absorb and hold moisture and provide a source of nourishment to mildew. That is not meant to reflect on acrylic flats, because that observation applies to all highly pigmented interior latex flats.

One good premise to work on is that you should not use the same coating in a relatively dry room that you use in a room with considerable moisture. For the latter, select one producing the hardest film, which means the one with the most resin. Pick a semigloss, or a high gloss, if this doesn't spoil decorating plans. Or select a so-called satin, or flat enamel such as P-32, which will be harder than a flat and yet won't be noticeably glossy.

Better still, if your exterior walls adjoining a sometimes moist room are constantly peeling, use a high performance epoxy, urethane, or rubber-based solvent-thinned coating for the interior. These will also be desirable if your shower area is besieged by stubborn mildew. If these are used, be particularly careful about surface preparation.

Interior Enamels. As a consumer you will probably be faced with selection of semigloss wall paints. Alkyds for years had an open field, but in recent years acrylic semigloss paints have proved formidable challengers; and now, polyvinyl acetate versions have come along, showing considerable promise.

Chart 6.1 shows that alkyds have better flow and leveling, which means they are easier to apply smoothly, than either of the other two, with acrylics not far behind. New versions of PVA are also satisfactory, despite results of the cited test.

Runniness of alkyds proved more bothersome than the other two, as indicated by the sagging test.

Alkyds (see P-36 and P-37) on the other hand, had better hiding, and measured up to acrylics in stain removal and wet adhesion to old enamels.

PVA offered shorter recoat time and quicker tack-free time, which means that it is less likely to pick up lint or dust than the others.

Acrylics (see P-38) had the least odor and shared with PVA the advantage of easy washup in water rather than solvent.

One or two paint manufacturers offer semigloss latex based on styrene acrylate, which showed up as a tough, wear-resistant material. In a test made by a British pigment manufacturer to assess the quality of American paints, it was found that a styrene acrylate semigloss paint survived 2,000 scrubs of a nylon-brushed scrubbing machine. An acrylic eggshell, with

103

Chart 6.1. Properties of Typical White Semigloss Paints.

	New 100% Acrylic Semigloss Paint	Solvent Alkyd Semigloss Paint	Early Latex* Semigloss Paint
Water cleanup	Yes	No	Yes
Open-time (length of time a coat of paint remains amenable to brushing)	15 minutes	15–20 minutes	5
Flow and leveling (0 = poor, 10 = perfect)	4	5	0
Sagging (running)	Very slight to none	Fair amount	None
Gloss (60°)	53 to 63	45	45
Hiding	Fair	Fair plus	Poor
Dry adhesion to old enamels	Good	Fair	Fair plus
Wet adhesion to old enamels (after 1 week air dry)	Good	Good	Poor
Odor	Very slight	Strong solvent	Fairly strong
Resistance to yellowing and embrittling	Good	Fair	Good
Tack-free time (77° F., 50% RH, low air circulation)	4 to 5 hrs.	3 to 5 hrs.	20–30 minutes
Recoat time (77° F., 50% RH, low air circulation)	4 to 5 hrs.	7 to 16 hrs.	1 hr.
Fire hazard	No	Yes	No
Print resistance (after 1 week air dry)	Very slight	Trace to none	None
Stain removal	Good	Good	Fair

Source: Rohm & Haas Co.

*Recently developed PVA latex semigloss paints are also regarded highly. However, acrylic versions have had such a head start that they are used by most companies. Acrylic semigloss enamels are widely used in hospitals and hotels because of their ease-of-cleaning and because unskilled maintenance staffs can apply them. Superior high-performance epoxies and urethanes usually require skilled painters.

less resin, showed slight erosion after 2,000 scrubs.

Interior wood surfaces, it should be noted, have certain characteristics that may at times require special treatment. We previously spoke about the need to use filler formulations on such large-pored cement materials as concrete or cinder blocks. Fillers of a different kind are needed for certain open-pored woods. Table 3.1 lists the kinds of wood found in various parts of American homes. Most of those requiring fillers are commonly used indoors.

These fillers are readily available. They are simple combinations of oil or varnish and fine silica. Fillers may be colored to match the wood to be treated. Consistency of the bought material may be adjusted to match porosity of the wood. Follow directions in thinning with ordinary mineral spirits. Apply with a stiff brush and wipe off, across the grain, with a dry rag. Nail heads and screws should be driven beneath the surface and filled over with putty or plastic wood after filling but before primer is used. Cracks should be filled in the same manner.

Dried fillers should be sanded flat before the entire area is painted.

7

New Objects from Old

Old furniture, toys, bicycles, railings, and awning supports, or just about any object that time and use have blemished can be rejuvenated, appearance-wise, by proper use of the right kind of paint.

Proper use involves the following steps:

1. Removal of old paint
2. Proper priming
3. Proper finishing

Removing old paint.   Three ways to remove old paint are by chemical stripping, sanding, and high heat.

Chemical stripping.   Numerous excellent proprietary products will remove coatings. Follow instructions and take normal care to avoid getting the material in eyes or on skin. Use of gloves is often desirable.

One precaution is to check the label, or ask the retailer, to determine if the recommended item will remove the kind of coating that must come off. It's easier to remove wall paint or furniture paint than to get baked enamel off a bicycle. Don't spend the money to buy a remover for baked enamel when a less expensive product will do. Let the retailer know what you want.

If possible, get a water-washable type because this permits water-hosing it off, with the aid of coarse steel wool.

Also, remember to check the softening of the finish to see if it is completely loosened. Sometimes the effectiveness stops before all finish is off. In that case, simply repeat until all is off.

Although some stores will try to sell you the water-washable as a matter of course, it's up to you to know when this should not be used. *Don't use a water-removable product if you are working on a wooden veneer, or an interior plywood that may not be water-resistant.* Warping

Fig. 7.1a *Steel wool entwined with ordinary string can be used for removing finish from spindles. Place steel wool over electrician's black tape. This provides a simple way to remove paint from curved surfaces.*

Fig. 7.1b *An old lollipop stick with steel wool wrapped around its tip lets you remove finish from carvings and intricate moldings.*

Fig. 7.1c *A fine steel brush should be used to remove debris from sanding and any other foreign matter present.*

or separating of plies may result. Don't use water if you expect to reach water-soluble stain and wood filler.

Sanding. For large surfaces, sanding by hand is time-consuming and fatiguing. Unless done very carefully, it may also damage the surface.

Using mechanical sanders poses the risk of oversanding and eating into smooth surfaces.

Either hand or mechanical sanding, however, has a role in cleaning up traces of paint left after chemical removal. (See Figs. 7.1a, b and c for simplified and efficient hand-sanding techniques.)

Heat. Devices can be bought or rented which blister an existing coat of paint without damaging the surface below.

Never use a torch or open flame source for paint removal. This is a serious fire hazard.

Many soldering iron sets include a tip intended for removing small areas of paint that may be hard to reach by chemical strippers or by sanding.

With any non-flame heat source, allow the coating to blister and soften sufficiently so that you can scrape it off with a steel scraping knife obtainable from any paint or hardware store. An old spackling or taping knife will serve the same purpose.

If the finish is such that chemical removers won't work, then heat is the only answer. Finishes likely to be stubborn enough to require heat are urethanes, epoxies and the tougher factory-finishes.

Special Notes. Remove all traces of chemical removers before finishing, or the final coat may be adversely affected. Remove all dust where sanding has been done. (See Fig. 7.2 for repair of small holes and dents.)

Selecting a Finish. Interior enamels described in Chapter 6 will serve under general conditions for most devices and furniture to be used indoors, and exterior enamels are suitable for exterior objects.

Wood Objects. Very often, however, special effects are desired, particularly where furniture is involved. Beautiful wood may be beneath heavy buildups of paint or varnish. Then, it may be desirable to use stains or varnishes that will take advantage of the wood's natural appearance.

Shellac, varnish and lacquer are used where clears are needed to let the wood show through. One mistake that homeowners frequently make is to use clear wax on a surface without a protective coating. Wax will protect the coating and help its sheen, but on bare wood it will be a prime dirt-gatherer. Once it works its way into the little fibres that constitute wood, it is very hard to remove; and it continues to gather dirt until it finally becomes necessary to sand down the surface to remove it. *So don't put wax on bare wood.*

Wood-fillers. Some woods are known as open-pore wood, and should be treated with fillers before coating so that a satisfactory surface will

*Fig. 7.2 Use stick shellac or wood putty to fill small holes. Gently smooth fill
material with a flexible spatula or knife. To smooth dents dampen a cloth, put over
dent and apply a hot iron until dent is out.*

result. Table 3-1 shows the relative stainability of wood and those woods
that need fillers. A filler is a varnish or vegetable oil containing a silicate.
This, in effect, blocks the porosity of the open-pore wood and prevents
lifting of the fibres in the wood.

Fillers are somewhat creamy in consistency, or may be paste-like.
They are brushed over the wood and, as they seem to be setting up,
the excess is wiped off, leaving pores filled and ready for varnish, stain,
or paint.

Fillers can be obtained to match just about any stain. Novelty effects
may be had by using a filler of one color and a stain of another.

Degrees of Clear Topcoat Gloss. To get a clear high gloss topcoat, you
have several choices, depending on how dusty the surroundings are. A
varnish will be easy to work with, but will take four hours or so to
dry hard enough to resist dust, and from about seven to 24 hours before
it can be recoated.

Lacquer and shellac dry almost immediately, so dust doesn't have
a chance to do harm. Both can yield rich gloss effects if polished between
coats.

For durability and toughness, varnish is the clear coating of choice.
Shellac mars when water reaches it, and should not be used on pieces
that are likely to be wet, such as tables where cocktails and water glasses
are placed.

Lacquer affords good protection, but it may chip or show cracks
more easily than the others.

A number of excellent varnishes based on the new synthetic resins
are available, depending on how much is to be spent. It is probable
that the extra cost of urethane and acrylic varnishes is thoroughly justified.

Avoid the mistake of using ordinary brushes for applying varnishes.
The extra cost of a special long-bristled, rather ample-bodied brush is
justified. A brush of this type permits holding enough varnish for long   109

strips in one direction and then similar ones in the other, like a cross-hatch that will be filled in by merging the intervening voids.

Don't let excesses build up in voids or odd places. Brushing out with dry bristles is necessary.

One advantage of using varnish is its slow setting up time, but this has the disadvantage of dust and lint pickup, which can be avoided by keeping painted objects in unused rooms.

Follow manufacturers' directions carefully as to drying time and recoat time. Remember some of the new synthetics dry faster and allow recoat the same day.

Natural look. If the look of natural wood, or moderately stained natural wood is desired, penetrating resins can be obtained that will protect without materially changing the natural or stained surface. The resulting natural look will endure in relation to the number of applied coats.

Simply pour on the finish and work it in with a soft pad as it enters the surface pores. Instructions will probably call for about 30 minutes of treatment for each coat and, depending on the product, an interval is prescribed before a second coat and possibly a third is applied.

An antiqued natural look is sometimes obtained by applying boiled linseed oil and turpentine over several days until the pores are saturated. Then rub the coated surface with sack cloth or similarly rough material and follow with ordinary linseed oil and rottenstone powdered and capable of being wiped in and away. After this has set about six to eight days and is hard enough, wax it to a desirable gloss.

Color Coats. Ordinary enamels can be used for color coats for wood. Preparation and application is similar to that used for any surface. For small areas, it is practicable to use spray cans, despite their extremely high cost per square foot. However, the freedom from mess justifies the cost, unless a large object is involved, in which case it may be better to rent a professional spray outfit and use far less expensive straight enamels.

For children's furniture or any object that will take a beating, highly durable epoxy enamels can be purchased. These are not as attractive as regular enamels. Another difficulty is that they usually come in two packages and must be mixed.

In recent years, antiquing kits have become so common that it is hardly necessary to learn the technique. If the reader wants to do it the hard way, he can buy an enamel of one color for his base coat and then have a clear, hard resin sealer as the topcoat. This permits addition of color pigments to achieve the antique effect desired. These are usually umber, or sienna, or any combination of these with other colors, including black.

110   The base coat is applied after roughing the under surface to assure

adhesion to the old coat. If desired, particularly if the surface is defaced and pocked, "distressing" can be achieved by pounding the face with a chain, stabbing it with a pointed knife, or whatever—before applying the base coat.

When the base is dry, put on the glaze topcoat. When this has set up and loses some of its sheen, rub from the center of the surface and work toward the outside, leaving the glaze wherever you wish. Usually, it is left in the indentations, the idea being to indicate that the "antiqued" piece has been worn away wherever the glaze is missing.

Unless the manufacturer indicates otherwise, it is necessary to protect the glaze with an over-coat varnish. Since this provides the protection, it is wise not to stint here. A polyurethane varnish should be applied two or three days after antiquing.

Metal Objects. Metal objects are mainly coated with opaque materials. Clears are used solely on copper and brass and rarely on precious metals.

A number of clear metallics are available at retail stores, with silicone resins probably offering longest protection. Acrylics are also offered. Since these are simple to obtain and use, they will not receive more than passing attention here.

Metal Primers. After preparing surfaces of metal objects in accord with Chapter 3, suitable primers should be applied. These must take into account the circumstances in which the object will be used. Metal to be used indoors with little or no exposure to water can be given ordinary alkyd metal primers as indicated in Chapter 6.

Railings, playground equipment, or bicycles that will be exposed to considerable weathering require corrosion-resistant primers containing special pigments. Most suitable primers can be obtained at paint stores, but those that are not in stores can be ordered from suppliers who serve industrial maintenance organizations.

Topcoats for Metal. With a proper primer, topcoats for metal can be selected on the same basis as other topcoats. The circumstances determine the choice. If ordinary circumstances prevail, an alkyd or latex topcoat with desirable degree of gloss can be selected.

However, if special considerations are involved, such as marine exposure, or if chemicals are likely to be splashed on or around the surface, or if it will be subjected to unusual blows or abrasion, then high performance coatings are likely. Since metal may involve a certain amount of flexing, it is probable that in many instances polyurethane coatings, preferably the two-package materials that must be combined at the site, will be best. These have an advantage over epoxies for exterior use—although the epoxies are also outstanding—because they have better color retention.

For repainting large objects, such as automobiles or boats, special   111 attention must be given to masking off trim, doors, etc. For these it is also desirable to use spray outfits, which may be rented. Special quick-dry lacquers can be obtained from auto supply and some paint stores. Detailed instructions for thinning and prevention of buildup should be followed carefully.

Refinishing Floors. After sanding down your floors, rub your hand over the surface to check for perfect smoothness. Parquet and block type floors require special care to avoid gouging because following the grain is impossible. Use a finer grade of paper than normal.

Remove all dust by vacuuming and clean with a dry absorbent mop before proceeding.

Oak or other open-grained wood floors need not be filled unless an ultra-smooth finish is desired. Staining may be done before filling, depending on manufacturers' illustrations. After staining, finish with a low-lustre clear varnish applied in one or two coats. Brush on liberally, first with the grain, followed by stroking across the grain. Do this for each small area at a time, going rapidly to the next area before the edges have set up. Brush from dry area to wet area. Apply second coat only after first is thoroughly dry. Sand lightly with very fine grit between coats.

New or Completely Stripped Floors. New floors or those completely stripped of finish may be coated with a clear wood seal or a penetrating finish. Apply freely and spread with a lambs' wool pad, cloth or brush. About 20 minutes is needed for penetration. Remove excess with a soft cloth before coating has had time to set. Observe if penetration is uniform before you wipe. If not uniform, wipe off excess anyway, then apply a second coat after the first is completely dry.

Allow at least three hours' drying time between coats. If desired, the penetrating sealer can be tinted by your dealer.

The finished floor should be protected from use at least overnight and then, if desired, wax may be applied for added protection and beauty.

Index